STAYING HAPPY, HEALTHY, AND HOT

Previous publications by Random House and Bantam Books:

Lovin' Touch
Lovin' Touch 2
Lovin' Touch 3
Lovin' Touch 4
Lovin' Touch 5

Previous publication by Subway Publications:

Together

STAYING HAPPY, HEALTHY, AND HOT

We're the Brand-New Louie Louie Generation

DICK SUMMER

iUniverse, Inc.
Bloomington

Staying Happy, Healthy, and Hot
We're the Brand-New Louie Louie Generation

iUniverse books may be ordered through booksellers or by contacting:

iUniverse
1663 Liberty Drive
Bloomington, IN 47403
www.iuniverse.com
1-800-Authors (1-800-288-4677)

Because of the dynamic nature of the Internet, any web addresses or links contained in this book may have changed since publication and may no longer be valid. The views expressed in this work are solely those of the author and do not necessarily reflect the views of the publisher, and the publisher hereby disclaims any responsibility for them.

Any people depicted in stock imagery provided by Thinkstock are models, and such images are being used for illustrative purposes only.

Certain stock imagery © Thinkstock.

ISBN: 978-1-4759-5560-6 (sc)
ISBN: 978-1-4759-5561-3 (hc)
ISBN: 978-1-4759-5562-0 (e)

Library of Congress Control Number: 2012919106

Printed in the United States of America

iUniverse rev. date: 10/15/2012

Contents

Foreward

A late August night, and you're sitting alone on the stoop in tee shirt and jeans. A bottle of Nedick's orange sweats at your side, and the Philco radio in the windowsill plays Sarah Vaughan so softly it stirs a warm breeze as the prettiest girl in the world turns the corner. Neighborhood kids in black sneakers run past her along the sidewalk chasing fireflies, while the guy across the street sprays a hose along the fins on his '57 Chevy. He turns, as you do, to watch the prettiest girl in the world walk slowly through the night air, her summer dress swishing against bare legs, her hair flowing like the waves at Coney Island. The yellow glow from a street lamp floods this beauty as though she were making her Broadway entrance. The guy across the street forgets his Chevy for the moment, and the garden hose aimlessly floods the driveway, washing the sidewalk where her feet—her perfect feet—will soon touch, if, indeed, angels ever reach Earth. Only, she glances at the water, then at him with a disapproving smile and turns toward you. You, the skinny kid on the stoop.

You stir, sunburned and sweaty—not so much from heat but from lust as she walks through swarms of uncapturable fireflies, exploding like stars around her. You glance at the Chevy guy, who's already lost out, and try to stand without tripping over your size 10 feet as this goddess in summer cotton slinks within kissing range, slowly opens her ruby mouth and whispers: "Mr. Summer, Dr. Gumline will see you now."

Poof! Sixty years flash into canned Barry Manilow music and worn golf magazines inside a suburban dentist's office where you don't want to be, surrounded in air-conditioned plastic that sucks the soul out of everyone who enters.

But you're a part of what Dick Summer calls the Louie-Louie Generation and you survive because, as Dick has shown his radio listeners for decades, life is but a dream. *Sha-boom.*

All it takes is a willingness to believe, as Dick does, in Tinker Bell, Santa Claus and the ability of words to not only capture time, but swirl them around inside your head where they can be analyzed from angles you've never considered. You're a guy or doll from the lost-and-found-again Louie-Louie Generation.

There's no age limit, no minimum number of years to enter this club, absolutely no ID card or test scores required. You just need to trust, as Dick does, in life's magic. Because only magic can explain why we fall in love, why baseball and nuns make us smile, or why for pilots like Dick and myself, growing older is like flying an airplane—the higher you go and the longer you stay aloft, the better the view.

Whether you're the guy on the stoop or the girl he thinks is the prettiest girl in the world, you're part of the Louie-Louie Generation. You've earned the right to pop open another

Nedick's for the Chevy guy across the street and, together, expose your minds to all of life's possibilities, because Dick Summer's Louie-Louie Generation might not remember where the car keys are, but it's grateful for having a car... somewhere. And it isn't really getting old. It's just now coming of age.

—Paul Berge

1-

The Times They Are A-Changin'

Once upon a time, in what now seems like a long, long, time ago, every generation lived in what they called the "old days." In those "old days," everybody got old. Worn out. Crunchy. Wrinkled. Yeeechh. That may be why they were called the "old days." But as Bob Dylan said, "The Times They Are A Changin'." So move over you Baby Boomers and Millennials, and all the rest of the generations of the past. We are the brand new Louie-Louie Generation, and we are "beyond your command."

We may not look like the people in the beer commercials anymore with their fancy abs and perky breasts, but we have lots of surprises in store for folks who think we're just left over chunks of luke warm meat. We know that he who dies with the most toys, wins. But our attitude is why envy that guy? He doesn't get to play with his toys. He's dead. So instead of getting grumpy and old, we're grateful that we have our own nice toys to play with. That's called the Louie Louie Generation attitude/gratitude connection. Here's how it works: Happiness helps us stay healthy. And happy healthy people are hot. And hot is sexy. And sexy makes us happy. It works. Most of the time.

This is mostly a collection of stories about how a Louie Louie Generation man and woman turn up the tingle in their everyday lives with a healthy jolt of the double 'tude—attitude and gratitude. It usually works. Not always. We're not perfect and that's good. Perfect gets boring pretty fast. And Louie Louie lads and ladies just aren't ever bored.

Louie Louie lads and ladies face a daily struggle for respect, recognition, and happiness against both the insolent forces of the sad and clueless Pimple People and the Drab and Dreadful Drones who have gone over to the dork side.

The world is overrun with Pimple People. Many of them wear their baseball caps sideways, drive spikes through their tongues, and wear their jeans low enough so that when they walk away they leave us with a parting nasty crack.

The Drab and Dreary Drones should know better. They've been around. But they just keep going around…and around…and around. They slouch through life, drenched in TV, slogging through soggy relationships, and settling for dimmed-down dreams. They wouldn't know a fun house if they lived in one.

Louie Louie-hood has lots of benefits. Louie Louie Generation guys are often the bedmates of choice of supermodels, lovely, lusty, lady chief executives, and Catherine Zeta-Jones look-alikes. That's because we treat our women with lots of love and lots of lovely lust, we have some pretty good life stories to tell, and we don't mind telling them, and many of us have paid off our nice cars and sometimes even our boats and private airplanes. We're guys with double doses of attitude and gratitude.

Louie Louie ladies know how to laugh and cry, love and lust, and cook… in every sense of the word. You'll enjoy watching a Louie Louie lady cooking comfortably at some high-powered job, hitting her Louie Louie guy on the shoulder while she laughs at his joke—that she's heard five times—while making sure the guy does the job exactly the way she wants it done.

And a Louie Louie lady on the prowl is a force of nature. A great example of that happened around here last Friday.

You should have seen her eyeing some guy sitting alone at an Applebee's bar. She put some perfume on her little lace hankie, slipped it into the guy's jacket pocket, smiled up at him, and walked away without a word. Naturally, he caught up with her and asked her what that was all about.

She just said, "It looks good in your pocket." Then she started asking if he went there often, and shook her head as if she couldn't hear and said, "It's noisy in here," and she leaned over toward him so she could hear his answer. That guy didn't stand a chance.

A Louie Louie lady was sitting at a table with a guy at lunch today. They were smiling and talking ... and she slowly slid her toe under his trouser cuff—nice and easy—and then tucked her foot back under her fanny. I don't know how women do that. But the nice thing is, they got up very abruptly, paid the check and left. Good.

Our "Virtual Founding Father" is Big Louie, his own bad self. We call him the Chief Mustard Cutter of our Louie Louie Generation. Big Louie's motto is, "The tingle is in the double 'tude, dude." And his tingle jingle is the song with a double title and a double dose of 'tude: "Louie Louie."

You're probably already a member of the Louie Louie Generation if you've been around long enough to have enjoyed making some of the same wonderfully bad mistakes that the rest of us have made. But your attitude and gratitude—your double 'tude—is far more important than your age for membership in our Generation. People who never heard of lava lamps, Frisbees, or hula hoops can be Louie Louie folks too, as long as they have that double 'tude.

The heroine of this book, and of my life, is "my Lady Wonder Wench." She is a first class Louie Louie lady. Sometimes she just sits over there on the couch and crosses her legs kind of high up on the thigh and lets one shoe slip off enough to show the sole of her foot.

Then she swings her foot back and forth a little. Oh yeah Louie-Louie ladies are very good at cooking.

This book is full of stories about how this Louie Louie lad and his "Lady Wonder Wench" are keeping our double 'tude-tingle working to keep us happy, healthy and hot. Usually. We've been together since that old black-and-white picture on the front cover was taken, so many years ago. And you'll see what the years haven't been able to take away from us in the pictures on the back cover.

Big Louie's words of wisdom are always worth remembering. For example: "As long as you've still got some moving parts, for cryin' out loud, move your parts."

2-

Louie-Louie-Lovin'

The smart guys in the white lab coats have now announced that they've figured out why men want to have sex with beautiful young women. After exhaustive research, they have decided that it's because we want to be sure that we spread our genes into the next generation. We want beautiful young women as mates, because they're the ones who are most likely to be healthy enough to see to it that our genes get where we want them to go.

Some smart guy doctor stood there on live TV the other night and actually said that with a straight face.

I think I can safely speak for my fellow Louie Louie Generation guys when I say: "There may be other reasons."

One of those reasons has quite accurately been summed up in the words, "EEE-HAA" which translates roughly to, "Oh thank you God, does that ever feel very good." Contrary to this new scientific theory, I'm here to tell you that shortly after I have experienced many of those EEE-HAA moments, I have prayed quite fervently to that same God, beseeching Him to drown every one of those pesky little genes in their own little gene pools. And I think I can safely say that my Lady Wonder Wench has joined me in that fervent prayer on more than one occasion.

There are lots of new theories about sex. My young friend Ty, a Louie Louie lad in training, says that the young women he knows all seem to be losing interest in sex. I don't think women are losing interest in sex at all. I think they're losing interest with the way Pimple People young guys go about EEE-HAA-ing. And those of us who are fortunate enough to be Louie Louie Generation guys are just delighted to see that, because we are totally dedicated to coming to the aid of suffering womanhood of all ages.

Young Pimple People guys often ignore, or at least pretend to ignore, any woman who is old enough to be finished wearing braces on her teeth. That's insulting, churlish, and wasteful. Fortunately, unattached Louie Louie Generation guys are always ready to carry the heavy burden of keeping as large a group of these young women as happy as possible. And attached Louie Louie guys like me are totally dedicated to keeping one woman happy, healthy, and hot. Why do you think I am always trying to talk my Lady Wonder Wench into letting me help her with her floor exercises? It has nothing to do with my genes and everything to do with her good health… more or less.

One of the many reasons that Louie Louie guys do well with women is because we are not afraid of them. We know we'll never understand them, and that's okay with us. Men and women are supposed to be different. That's good. And most important of all, we really like women. Pimple People guys don't understand that men are never going to understand women; but that's okay … it has always been that way and the race has survived, so it's not something to fear. But Pimple People guys just never learn that lesson. They keep trying and failing; and that scares them. You simply can't really like women if they scare you.

We, on the other hand, understand that women make the social rules in our society, and we understand that one of the very famous rules is: "Men are not allowed to know exactly what any of the rules are." But we know we can get around problems like that as long as we have our American Freedom of Speech. We're allowed to talk to anybody. So we'll often walk right up to a beautiful woman of any age and say something like, "May I tell you something in complete confidence?" That gets any woman's attention and usually makes her lean in toward us and smile, and then we just very simply say something like, "You are very beautiful."

We've been around. We know that only 20 percent of American women think they're beautiful. It's obvious to us that's a very lowball figure. Walk down any American street and look around—while trying to avoid leaving teeth marks on a tree when you bump into it because some passing beautiful woman takes your mind off your mind.

And we also know that every woman looks in the mirror before she goes out and fiddles and fixes till she can honestly say, "Hey, I look pretty good." And we're just delighted to re-enforce her positive feelings. Because that gets us at least a smile. Sometimes more.

In my case, I am totally devoted to protecting my Lady Wonder Wench from the lesser affections of younger men. When she gets dressed to go out with me, I never miss the opportunity to smile appreciatively, bow a little in her direction, and say something low and warm like, "Wow." That makes her glow. Attitude/gratitude. Happy, healthy and hot.

I love seeing Louie-Louie ladies glowing. But sometimes they forget they can do that because the media is all hung up on the pictures, careers, and love lives of Pimple People Princessess, who still haven't gotten over chasing guys who are really neat dancers.

So Big Louie, his own bad self, always reminds his guys that a warm and well placed "Wow" is a wonderful way to turn on a Louie-Louie's lady's glow.

I wonder how long it will take the smart guys in the white lab coats to figure out that there's more to sex than spreading our genes.

When they recover from all their exhaustive research, they may even discover the awesome power of the word "Wow." Our Louie-Louie ladies understand it very well. They know that they glow when we say "Wow." They like glowing. Because they also know that "Wow" is really our sophisticated, worldly, gentlemanly way of saying "EEE-HAA."

And EEE-HAA has nothing at all to do with genes.

3-

I Taste Bad

I must taste bad. Especially to mosquitos. They simply don't bother me. My Lady Wonder Wench is in the bathroom right now, applying itch ointment to a mountain of mosquito bites in surprisingly personal places. She obviously tastes good. Which figures, when you look at her. But that makes her a human salad bar for mosquitoes.

There is a difference between tasting bad and bad taste. Tasting bad makes you mosquito proof, keeps you from sucking your thumb when it's time to write a check for your income tax, and keeps elderly-aunt kisses to a minimum when you are a child. Bad taste is wearing a nose ring with bifocals, spiked hair near a bald spot, and short shorts with varicose veins. Big Louie, his own bad self, always says, "Don't sweat that stuff. Just wear whatever you can still button that doesn't itch and can still pass the sniff test. If you want to wear a thong with your Depends, go for it." That's bad taste.

I think the words used in most advertising for Louie Louie Generation people are certainly in bad taste: regularity, insomnia, dentures, arthritis, indigestion, erectile dysfunction. That last one is not only in bad taste, it's confusing. If you watch the commercial, it seems to be about a guy who went to see Alice, his girlfriend, but certain of his bodily parts must have fallen asleep while they were supposed to be paying attention, so he and Alice spent the evening together just soaking in separate bath tubs. Makes no sense to me. Go see Alice yourself and see if you can figure it out.

When is the last time you saw advertising for us Louie-Louie Generation folks with words like designer jeans, beer, health club, casino, skiing, sexy beaches, or fun for the whole family? Actually, the truth is, nothing in life is fun for the whole family. I think that's why some guys never have families. Priests aren't allowed to have families. But what kind of life is that? You give up your sex life, and then every Saturday night people come and tell you about theirs in confession. Must drive priests nuts.

I could never figure out why some things are considered in bad taste. Sticking your tongue out at somebody, for example. Your tongue is a very intimate part of your body. Some French-speaking people use it to add a significant level of eroticism to their kisses. It seems to me that showing someone such an intimate part of your body should be considered kind of sexy. Guys should be telling their buddies, "Hey I went to see Alice, my girlfriend last night, and she let me see her tongue. She started rubbing it around on the tips of her teeth, and then in a fit of passion, she tossed her head back and stuck it right out at me."

Passing wind is considered to be in such bad taste that you can't even discuss it in polite company—which is silly for several reasons. A fart has no taste at all. It just smells bad. But lord, it feels so good. It's even better than sneezing. My Lady Wonder Wench doesn't like to sneeze. But I do. I don't like coughing, but I sometimes sneak peeks at a bright light just to make myself sneeze. I am also an enthusiastic consumer of baked beans.

Picking your teeth is considered to be in bad taste. But brushing your teeth gets you a gold star.

Singing at the table is out. Why? There are great drinking songs; why aren't there any great eating songs? When you were a kid, how often did you hear, "No, you mustn't sing at the table. Just shut your mouth and eat"? How are we supposed to do that? "Don't chew with your mouth open, and for God's sake, don't blow on the soup either." How come we can blow on a birthday cake's candles, but we can't blow on our soup?

There's a time and a place for good taste. But there are some things that are much more important than good taste.

Good taste is never more strictly observed than at a military funeral. I had a friend by the name of Joe, who now rests in peace in the Calverton, New York, Military cemetery. Joe was a very well-known writer, a real friend, and a bit of a rascal. He liked doing weird things. Things that were in terribly bad taste. For example, one night he loaded a water pistol with warm water, put it in his pocket, and stumbled into a bar pretending he was drunk. He leaned against one of the other guys at the bar and pulled the trigger on the water pistol, sending a sudden stream of warm water down the guy's pants. I'm not sure how he got out of there alive. But that was Joe.

On the very sad day when he was laid to rest, my Lady and I took part in a moment of something that some people would say was in terribly bad taste. But it was a moment I'll never forget.

There was an honor-guard rifle salute, befitting Joe's honorable and courageous service in the U.S. Army. When the last shots were fired, a quick shaft of sunlight reflected from a bugle's brightly burnished brass as a soldier—standing tall, at attention—played taps. Such a lonely sound, taps: precise, respectful, tearfully final. Day is done. Rest in peace. The flag was folded and presented to Joe's widow. White gloves. Deadly silence. Most respectful good taste.

But then, when the coffin was lowered into the ground, as Joe had requested in his will, the bugler added a few bars of Joe's favorite song. It was in terribly bad taste. But we sang along, as Joe wanted us to do.

We all stood together there, in the bright sunlight, three of his ex-wives and a small group of his friends, including my Lady and me, all so sad, holding hands and huddled together. And we sang: "M-I-C … We'll see you again some day… K-E-Y … Why? Because we loved you. M-O-U-S-E."

It was in terrible taste. But under the tears some of us were finally able to smile. There were even a couple of quiet laughs. Joe loved laughs. One last laugh together is a good way to remember a friend.

Forever.

4-

Mano-a-Mouse-o

L et me take you back to very early this morning; 4:18 a.m. to be exact. I know because I caught a glimpse of the digital alarm clock on the dresser. I was in the middle of a dream that seemed to have something to do with Catherine Zeta-Jones. I didn't even notice my Lady Wonder Wench getting out of bed and going for a potty break. But just as Catherine Zeta was smiling seductively and introducing me to her twin sister in my dream, Lady W. W. cut loose with a shriek that must have cracked windows all the way to Greg's house down the block.

Without even waiting for instructions from my brain, my legs did about a quarter of a mile in 1.2 seconds because I was lying on my side. But in the process, somehow one foot hit the floor, which, of course, caused me to run right into Mr. Wall. That woke me up enough to realize that my L. W.W. had either seen an asteroid the size of Asia hurtling directly toward us, the New York Mets had blown another pennant race, or there was a mouse loose somewhere within our zip code.

The bathroom door slammed and a pink streak flashed into the bedroom and up onto a chair. It was pretty obvious that Mrs. Wench

13

was considering climbing up to an even safer position on top of her dresser. Now, as a Louie Louie Generation guy I've been around long enough to know that trying to calm a woman down with words while she is trying to climb up on her dresser is not only not going to work, it's like trying to put out a kitchen fire with a can of gasoline. It was obviously time for action. I was going to have to go head-to-jaws with the mouse. Mano-a-mouse-o. Me against Mickey. And it wasn't going to be a catch and release—Mrs. Wench was calling for a scalp. Mickey had to go down.

I quickly slipped on my slippers and pulled on some shorts to protect my most vulnerable parts from possible retaliation on the part of the mouse, grabbed my baseball glove from the top of the closet, and went on the attack.

I opened the bathroom door just a crack, so he couldn't come running out (and up my leg), and there he was, trying to hide behind the bathroom scale: about two inches long, probably weighing in at three or four ounces, two malevolent red eyes gleaming, fangs bared, tail thrashing back and forth in anticipation of the battle. My plan was to distract him by talking to him while my baseball-glove hand sneaked around behind him for the grab.

Things were going well. I was bent down just a couple of feet from the snarling mini-monster, my baseball glove just inches away from a catch, when he suddenly jumped—vertically—straight up into the air a good two feet, right at my face as if he were on the attack. I did a quick retreat, and tripped over the spare toilet paper holder and landed on my fanny. The mouse countered by jumping behind the wicker laundry basket. I slowly and carefully pulled the basket away from the wall. I could see him lurking, looking up at me.

And then he started squeaking. He was issuing a challenge. I swear he was going Mouse-o-a-Mano and he wasn't planning on losing. Obviously I wasn't going to take that. I shoved the basket back against the wall hard because I figured I'd flatten him there.

But he was too fast for me. He streaked around into the empty broom closet.

So I started thinking, "Yeah, oh yeah. Thank you, Mr. Mouse, I'll just grab a broom and clock you with it." And POW! He jumped up at me again, and I tripped on the rug and fell on my fanny again. I could hear him squeaking, and I swear he was laughing at me. He was laughing at me! He was looking at me from behind the toilet plunger and laughing.

He was obviously way too fast for me to catch him and hit him. So I was thinking I've got to slow him down. How do I do that? Then I saw a can of hair spray in the closet, and I remember when I was watching King Kong and thinking that if only those guys had a big enough can of hair spray, they could have spritzed it on that big hairy guy's fur and that would slow down even King Kong.

So there I was, Mano-a-Mouse-o, armed with a baseball glove on one hand and a can of hair spray in the other. And looking backward, that's a pretty weird picture, I will admit. By this time he was back, crouched behind the scale again. So I cut loose a spritz of spray, and I got him.

I saw him kind of blink and he jumped again—right over me— and he disappeared. I mean he completely disappeared. He was Mickey Mouse with Michael Jordan moves. I looked everywhere, and I couldn't find him. I even looked in the medicine closet. He was gone. But I knew he was too much of a battler to give up. I knew he'd be back. So this morning, I got some weapons of mouse destruction, some poison and a couple of traps, and I put them around the house.

It used to be that you could get those little wooden mousetraps or some mouse poison if you preferred. But I guess mouse terrorism must be on the rise around here, because the weapons-of-mouse-destruction shelves at the hardware store are bulging with what can only be called twenty-first-century technology. There's even a trap that looks like a little dollhouse. You lure the mouse in there with a little smear of peanut butter, or a slice of cheese, or maybe a seductively posed 3-D picture of Minnie Mouse. Anyway, he goes in there and an electric charge does him in as he passes through the doorway. (Batteries not included.) Lots of the traps are designed so you don't even have to see the poor little guy. You just throw the trap and the corpus delicti away. Not very sportsmanlike, if you ask me.

But … I put some traps and some poison around the house, and sure enough, right after lunch, I went down to the computer room, and there he was. Motionless. Sprawled out on the carpet. Dead. I guess I should have felt victorious. But I couldn't help thinking of the contrast here. He's about three ounces by three inches. I'm about five ten and 180 pounds. And he battled me to at least a draw. I couldn't beat him when it was just Mano-a-Mouse-o. I had to bring in cowardly weapons of mouse destruction to do the job.

I know I didn't have much choice if I was going to pry my Lady Wonder Wench off the dresser. But I kept thinking about when I was a kid, and how much fun I had with the story about "Hickory dickory dock, the mouse ran up the clock." And how I always told our kids the story about "'Twas the night before Christmas and all through the house, not a creature was stirring, not even a mouse." And a long time ago, when television sets had rabbit ears, they also had those mouse ears that Annette Funicello wore on her head.

So good night, Mr. Mouse. Sleep easy. You did good. You didn't beat me, but I didn't beat you either. Your mama would be proud. Even I'm proud of you. You did good.

5-

Click Here

M embership in the Louie Louie Generation can mean some big changes in the way we lead our lives. And as you know, big changes are almost always built one little change at a time. The Chrysler building is a good example of that. It's one of New York's biggest skyscrapers. And it's mostly built of bricks. A bunch of guys just put one little brick on top of another little brick until they got quite a view. Even man-mountain Shaq O'Neil is the result of one little microscopic egg sharing kind of a hot-tub experience with a heavy-breathing little sperm who managed to wriggle out of his Speedo for the occasion. And think of the big effect of the little clicks on your TV remote. They change the channels you're watching from PBS to Saturday Night Live.

It was an amazing parade of tiny clicks that changed my personal channel to the one that features the lady in my life. I call her my Lady Wonder Wench.

Here's what happened: Santa brought me a portable radio when I was about seven. (Click.) I immediately became a disc jockey in training. I listened to William B. Williams on WNEW and Big Wilson on WNBC in New York, and I loved it. WNEW and WNBC are big league stations. The radio business is like baseball—you start in the minors and work your way up. I worked my way up to WIBC in Indianapolis, which is a top-level triple-A kind of station. (Click) And then, for some reason, Al Heacock, the Program Director at WBZ in Boston, fished around in a big box of audition tapes and came up with mine. He liked it. (Click.) I was in the majors. And I was just a few clicks away from meeting my Lady.

She wanted to be a veterinarian when she was seven. But her family didn't have the money to send her to school for that. (Click.) So she became a secretary—a very good one. (Click.) She got a good job after high school as a secretary in a law office. A good job, but no tingle. (Click.) Her mother listened to WBZ all the time. (Click.) They aired a commercial for a job opening one morning. (Click.) Her mom heard it and challenged my Lady to try for it. (Click.) She did. And she won.

But WBZ was a big station. My Lady worked during regular business hours. I was the all-night disc jockey. We never saw each other. Two more tiny clicks had to happen to make it work.

Nobody at a radio station pays much attention to the all-night disc jockey. Everybody is asleep when he's on the air. But one evening, all the WBZ deejays played a charity basketball game, and the station's secretaries went to the game to be our cheerleaders. Almost all of them cheered for the daytime guys. But on the few occasions that I did anything right, I heard one lovely, lusty cheer coming from a beautiful blue-eyed secretary with dangerous curves and such an amazing smile. (Click.)

I've worked at bigger stations: WNEW and WNBC in New York, which were the stations I listened to on my little transistor radio when I was a kid. But WBZ is one of the most powerful stations in the country. I was getting sacks full of mail every night and I wanted to try to answer it. So I asked the head secretary if any of her staff would like to earn a few extra bucks helping me out with the mail.

Guess who showed up for the gig? (Click.)

6-

The Godless Communist Chinese Reality TV Show

B ig Louie always says, "When things are beginning to make you sweat, and frustration levels are mountin', don't do stuff you'll later regret, cool down your head in your mental fun fountain." I dunked my head in my fun fountain today and found a surprise floating around in there. Here's what happened:

It was a sweaty day yesterday, and I felt like I was starring in one of the leading reality TV shows on some government-run Godless Communist Chinese Television Network. It was exhausting. Loosely translated, the show would probably be called, "Tune In and Laugh at American Guys Trying to Put Together the Stuff We Make ... Ha, Ha." It's an endless series of satellite shots that zoom in on American guys like me putting together three-person porch swing sets imported from China.

It's the kind of swing that Kevin Costner and Susan Sarandon are sitting on at the end of the movie Bull Durham, except that it's a three-seater. Why is it a three-seater? Could it be that they're trying to mess up American morale by threatening to send commie-commissar chaperones to screw up our romantic summer evenings on a porch swing?

Besides the swing set in my back yard, and the barbecue grill on my back deck, some ordinary Chinese guy made the little Christmas tree lights that I string on my tree every year. Chances are, he doesn't really know what Christmas is, or why little lights have anything to do with it. He's just showing up for work every day and putting in his ten or twelve hours sticking those little bulbs in those tiny sockets.

His fingers must hurt by the time he leaves the factory, and on the way home, he breathes that dirty air that we all saw during the Olympics a few years ago. I started thinking it's really too bad he doesn't know how it feels to just toss a hamburger on a grill and have a bunch of friends over on the Chinese version of our Fourth of July, celebrating freedom by drinking beer, laughing, telling corny jokes, and watching the fireworks at night. The Chinese guy's neighbor probably made those fireworks.

But then I realized that the little Chinese guy doesn't have a holiday like our Fourth of July. He doesn't have our kind of fun. He doesn't have our kind of freedom. It's just not something he's probably going to understand. At least not right now.

The Chinese government has been rattling some rockets lately, and all our talk show hosts and other "concerned experts" have their shorts tied up pretty tight. But I was just thinking about that ordinary Chinese guy, working his fanny off to make the nut that's sitting somewhere in the tall grass behind my home. And I started thinking about what Big Louie, his own bad self always says: "Watch out, because Non-Judgment Day is coming."

So, little ordinary Chinese guy who made the bolt that fits the nut I lost, maybe you'd like to know that my Lady Wonder Wench and I got to watch the fireflies last night, rocking gently back and forth on the swing set that you made and I put together. My Lady Wonder Wench likes her burgers almost raw …I like mine medium… and that barbecue grill you made and I put together sizzles them just right. If you lived around here, I'd be glad to flip one for you too. I know where I can get some good Chinese Tsingtao beer and there's plenty of room for it in the cooler. American guys like to share stuff like that.

And I hope you someday get to walk into a room filled with the scent of a real Christmas tree, see the lights you made, listen to songs called "Jingle Bells" and "Silent Night," and hear the little kids laughing and tearing the pretty paper off their presents. I think you'd like that. I know the guy down the block from you probably made the paper—and the toy inside. Please thank him for us.

And while you're tuned in and laughing at us American guys trying to put together the stuff you made, there are some things you should understand: First of all, laugh all you want. We like laughs. We especially like laughing at the jokes we make about ourselves. Second, you know those Christmas lights you made? Well Christmas is a celebration that has to do with the birth of Christ…among other things. We don't have to celebrate Christmas, and we don't have to follow a religion. But we can if that's what we want to do. It's up to us. That's freedom. We love freedom. I think you'd like it too. I think you'd also like hot hamburgers and cold beer. And air that has lots of sunshine in it.

Maybe most of all, I'd like you to know that American guys respect people who know how to work till their fingers hurt, because we know how to do that too. I was sipping some Won-Ton soup yesterday, and thinking how neat it would be if some day we could get together after work, and do some celebrating together.

7-

Sir Richard and the Lance of Doom

I was sitting in my big, comfortable, black-leather poppa chair in my living room last night, watching a stinkbug crawling up the wall toward the ceiling. I knew that if I mentioned this to my Lady Wonder Wench, who was sitting in her usual spot on the couch—right under the bug—she would run right out of her socks into the kitchen, and she'd trip and hurt herself. I didn't want that to happen. On the other hand, I was a bit concerned that if I didn't tell her about it, the bug might fall down from the ceiling and land in her lap, in which case she would skip the running part, pull a Star Trek move, and just kind of beam herself into some parallel universe, leaving only her T-shirt, skirt, socks, and hair behind on the couch, as sad reminders of the wonderful, sexy, happy life we had when she lived here in this universe with me.

Fortunately, something she was cooking started making a strange hissing sound, so she got up gracefully and walked into the kitchen to quiet it down, giving me the opportunity to spring into action. I started to climb up on the couch pillows, which is a delicate balancing act. Try it if you don't think so. You find yourself trying to hang on to the wall, which doesn't really work. Regardless of the danger, I knew I had to climb up on the back of the couch to reach the bug. For some reason, it seemed like a good idea to grab a picture frame with my left hand, to help me pull my other foot up so I could stand on the back of the couch with a yardstick in my hand and I could give the bug a deadly thwap. I swung—and missed. The picture frame broke, I lost my balance and fell down on her new end table, breaking a leg—the table's, not mine.

As my Lady's knight in shining armor, it was, to say the least, a smudge on my escutcheon.

For those of you who may never have seen an actual escutcheon, it's a knight's shield where he puts his coat of arms, as opposed to his tin coat, which is where he puts his real arms so they won't get cut. Those knights had lots of arms. Because they were all once adolescent boys.

As you know, when girls become adolescent, they develop breasts. And according to many ladies who have been through the process, when boys become adolescent, they see those new developments. And through the simple process of evolution, and heavily humming hormones, those boys quickly develop extra hands. A lot of extra hands. And of course they then need a lot of extra arms on which to hang those hands. I guess that's why, when the military was made up of only guys, we began calling them an "Army." (Sorry…no… I'm not really sorry. I got kind of a kick out of that one.)

Stinkbugs are smart. I think they send out scouts to see how tall you are. That way, when they report back, the rest of the bug brigade knows exactly how high they can sit on our walls. They keep just out of the reach of those of us who want to be our Ladies' knights in shining armor, thereby luring us into climbing on the backs of our couches, hanging onto walls, falling off, and damaging both our escutcheons and our furniture. I swear I heard that damn little bug giggle when I hit the floor.

But we knights don't just lie on our fannies on the floor when we're insulted like that. No, sir. We usually scramble to our feet, hit our heads on a lamp, knock over a cup of coffee that was sitting on our laptop computer, and proclaim some very naughty words that Greg and Cindy, our neighbors all the way down the block, probably haven't heard since they were in the fifth grade … and going through adolescence together.

Of course, when all else fails, sometimes one of us knights actually allows a thought to get through the helmet perched on top of all that shining armor. I was standing there, looking at a broom stick, just minding its own business, standing in the corner. I was going to use it in case a stickball game broke out when my buddy Jim came to visit.

"Sir Richard," I sayeth unto myself, "That looketh like a knight in shining armor's lance." And so it did. And so it was that I took some duct tape, wrapped it sticky side out at the top of the lance and invented Sir Richard's Lance of Doom. Mr. Bug didn't understand. But with one carefully aimed flick of the wrist, Sir Richard took his revenge. Revenge can be very sweet.

Big Louie always reminds us Louie-Louie Generation guys that there are lots of ways besides killing bugs and opening jars to be your lady's knight in shining armor. For example, touch her hair when you pass her chair. Kiss her on the forehead. Listen to her. Keep her secrets. Take her out to dinner. Call her. Make sure your friends know how proud you are that she's your girl. Tell her she's beautiful. Make her feel safe with you. Dance with her, even if you're not a good dancer. Sing to her, even if you sing off-key. Kiss her in the rain. Hold her hand. Write her quick love notes. Remember her birthday and the day you first met. Remember her favorite color. Touch her cheek. Tell her she's your star. If she must cry, make sure you always have room for her in your arms. Bring her flowers. Let her fall asleep in your arms. Give her a piggy-back ride. Look into her eyes for a full minute and then slowly smile. If you love her, tell her. Tell her how wonderful it is that she shares such a sexy, happy life with you. Tell her how glad you are that she lives here in this universe with you. Promise her that she'll never have to beam herself out of the universe you share because of some stinkbug—because you now have the lance of doom, and you know how to use it. Double 'tude her. Give her your personal, very special attitude with gratitude. Keep her happy, healthy and hot.

I'll bet, if you do that, she'll give you her T-shirt to tie on your helmet the next time you go into one of life's real battles. I'll also bet that the T-shirt will still be nice and warm. Maybe even hot.

And so will you.

8-

E Pluribus Unum

Sometimes when you go to a ball game, you get more than a game, a hot dog, and a beer. Sometimes you get a shot in the gut that makes you feel so good, so proud.

It was at a New York Mets spring training game when the PA announcer asked everyone to "stand and honor America, as eight-year-old Grace [somebody] sings our national anthem."

I don't remember her last name. I wish I did. She walked out behind home plate and stood in front of probably six thousand people in all her four-foot-something, maybe ninety-pounds worth of little-girl splendor. She was probably the only person in the stadium wearing a dress. Pink, I think, with a little yellow bow on top.

Lady Wonder Wench and I stood up, put our hot dogs on our seats, and put our hands over our hearts. Little Grace took a deep breath and started to sing.

"Oh say can you see, by the dawn's early light ..." It was a little girl's voice but it had a hint that in a few years it might sound a bit like the late, great Whitney Houston ... but not yet.

"What so proudly we hail, at the twilight's last gleaming …" I started thinking about how proud my Lady and I are of our two little girls, grown-up women now, with their own kids.

"Whose broad stripes and bright stars, through the perilous fight, o'er the ramparts we watched were so gallantly streaming …" The old guy in the row in front of me had one arm around his wife, and his other hand was holding a very ancient baseball cap over his heart. The cap said, "Army." It was probably circa Korea or maybe even W.W. 2. He stood as straight and tall and proud as my dad used to stand.

"And the rockets' red glare, the bombs bursting in air…" The old guy and his wife began singing along with Grace, very quietly and a little off-key, but singing. And Lady Wonder Wench started singing along with them. Singing and crying. Softly. I knew she was thinking about her brother Bob. His simple white cross stands in the sand behind Otis Air Force Base on Cape Cod.

"Gave proof through the night that our flag was still there …" More and more of the people around us started singing, very quietly and a little off-key, but singing… together.

"Oh, say, does that star-spangled banner yet wave …" All of us were singing now. Very quietly and still a little off-key. but singing. All of us. All around the field.

"O'er the land of the free …" Even I was singing. Quietly. Off-key, I guess. But singing—and thinking about my uncle Joe, the World War 2 B-17 navigator, and my brother Geoff, who did a second US Army tour in Vietnam because he knew the experience he got the first time around would save a couple of buddies. He was right. It cost him a chunk of his leg, but he never talks about his Purple Heart or his Bronze Star.

"…And the home of the brave." We all sang it together, quietly and a little off-key: little Grace, the old guy and his wife, my Lady Wonder Wench, me with my jacket that says Brooklyn across the front, and about six thousand other people who just came to enjoy a baseball game together.

It wasn't a huge majestic sound. It was really kind of quiet and a little off-key. But it was all of us together. I don't think any of us expected that.

There was an almost embarrassed moment of stunned silence. Then someone in the bleachers cut loose with one of those long, loud, two-fingers-between-the-teeth whistles, and the place exploded with applause and laughs, more than a few tears, and so much pride—so much pride we all felt at that moment. Together.

It was an e pluribus unum moment: out of many, one. That's more than just a slogan on our money. It's what makes us unique. It's what makes us so powerful. No nation has ever done what we do on the scale that we're doing it. No country anywhere near our size, with our power, our wealth, our thrust, has ever been governed by its own people. There have been kings and dictators who have successfully ruled over their people. But here, we are our own rulers. We are a magnificent human experiment in progress.

Then a little guy by the name of Tyler threw out the ceremonial first pitch. Tyler looked like about six years old. He was wearing a Little League uniform and a fiercely determined look on his face. He threw from a full windup. And he threw a strike. The crowd gave him a big cheer. Then the announcer mentioned that Tyler was a representative of The Make a Wish Foundation. And the crowd was quiet for a moment, and then they went nuts.

As you may know, The Make-A-Wish Foundation is an organization devoted to helping make at least one wish come true for kids, like little Tyler, who are probably going to die. Soon. But little Tyler had only one thing on his mind. He went out there and threw his strike. He didn't let the fact that he wasn't going to throw many more of them stop him. He just rared back and fired his pitch.

That song we sang together just before the baseball game—the one about the bright stars and the broad stripes and the perilous night—ends with a question to which I think Francis Scott Key really wished he knew the answer all those years ago. "Oh say does that star-spangled banner yet wave, o'er the land of the free and the home of the brave?"

My shot in the gut answer is yes. As long as we have kids like Amazing Grace and Tough Tyler. And as long as we have a bunch of ball parks full of Americans who are proud to stand up and sing that song about America. Even if we're all singing in different keys. As long as we're still singing it together.

9-

The Princess and the Frog

My Lady Wonder Wench has been my girlfriend for a long time. I don't even remember what my opening line was with her. I don't think I had one. It was so long ago that you could still sometimes actually hear "Louie Louie" on the radio. That's a long time ago.

So I started wondering about what I could use for an opening line to start a conversation with some other girl if, after all these years, my Lady Wonder Wench finally realizes that no matter how nicely she kisses me and makes a wish I'm not going to turn into a prince, and so she takes off with somebody like George Clooney. As an experiment, I ran some opening lines past her at dinner a few weeks ago. When she heard most of them, she just looked at me and said, "Huh?"

Huh is an interesting word that I think may have been invented once upon a time, many years ago, when a beautiful princess kissed a frog and turned him into a handsome prince. Now, it doesn't say so in the book, but if you're a Louie Louie generation parent, you've heard some pretty fancy stories from your own kids, so you will understand that when the princess's mother showed up in the morning and found this strange guy in the bedroom with her daughter—and the girl explained, "He's a magic prince, and he just popped out after I kissed a frog"—I'm willing to bet that "Huh?" might have been one of the first things her mom said. Don't you think?

I tried lots of opening lines on my Lady Wonder Wench in this experiment.

"I may not be a genie, but I can make your dreams come true."

"I'm not really this tall; I'm sitting on my wallet … my dear." (*My dear* always sounds so deliciously sleazy to me.)

"Hi. I'm Mr. Right, and somebody said you were looking for me."

I tried lots of lines, but only one worked.

It's hard for a guy to come up with an opening line that's good enough to get a kiss from a pretty girl, let alone an invitation to her bedroom, even at a singles bar. But think about that frog. He did it. What a clever guy. He must have skipped right past the, "What's your sign?" stuff, and come up with a real winner. I'll bet he popped a little fly breath mint into his mouth, hopped right up into the girl's lap, looked her straight in the eye, and seductively said, "*Ribbit.*"

Next time you're in a singles bar, I'll bet you will get any girl's attention if you pop a breath mint, jump into her lap, look her right in the eye, and seductively say, "*Ribbit.*"

I've heard worse opening lines.

"Your eyes are as blue as my toilet water at home. (Bleeech.)

"*Poof!* … I'm here. Now what are your other two wishes?" At least that's a little clever, but you're really leaving yourself open for some nasty comebacks with that one.

Oh yeah, the only line that actually worked with my Lady Wonder Wench was "How would you like a flight in my little airplane, my dear?" That worked. Sort of.

We went for a flight that night, as we have many nights. But no matter how carefully I explain why I put an autopilot in the plane, she still doesn't seem to understand the concept of the Mile-High Club.

Next time, I'll have to turn up the intercom, look her right in the eye, and whisper "*Ribbit.*" I'll bet that will make the guys at Air Traffic Control say, "Huh?"

10-

She's Saving His Seat

I'm back from vacation with a bit of a tan, a substantially thinner wallet, and a head full of vacation snapshots to run past you.

Here's one: we were walking along the beach, and all of a sudden, a shadow rippled across the sand and then flew out into the bay. It was a big pelican coming in for a water-ski landing, feet first. He settled into the water, looked around at the people on the beach, and tossed his head as if he expected at least a quick cheer for his performance. I gave him a short burst of applause.

Here's another: An old-time Chevy station wagon pulled into that same beach's parking lot, with a license plate that expresses a deeply felt urge for many a Louie Louie Generation lad and lass. It said, "I-Gotta-P."

And speaking of pee-ing, (there is a connection) the new Budweiser slogan is "Grab some buds." That's okay on their TV commercials. But they probably didn't think about how that slogan would look when it is proudly displayed on the tight T-shirts of the young ladies selling their beer at the ballpark. "Grab some buds." I don't know. It sure got my attention—which got a few slightly unladylike comments from my Lady Wonder Wench.

Then there's a snapshot that I think I'll frame and keep somewhere very close to where I live. We were taking a little walk in the park across the street from our hotel, and we saw an old guy sitting on a park bench, just sitting—not even reading—just sitting and watching the people walk by. As we walked past, I noticed a brass plaque on the bench. It said, "In memory of Amelia, my wife and my best friend. She's saving me a seat now." I didn't let go of my Lady's hand for quite a while.

Everything looks different when you're on vacation. I've noticed that even the guy in my shaving mirror sometimes looks a little different when I'm on vacation. The first morning we were there, he was waiting for me—the guy in my mirror. He was happy to see me, because he had been up taking care of me all night while I was sleeping, and it was a long night. I started thinking about him. Was he on vacation too? Then I started thinking, I'm looking at retirement pretty soon. And he's got to know that. And I started wondering if that guy in the mirror is as scared as I am that he may be suddenly finished with the daily life-long process of "getting ahead" and trying to make a living.

And how about the other end of his life? The first times. What kind of secret celebration did he enjoy the first time his mom let him comb his own hair before he went to school? How big were the monsters that prowled around in the attic when he was home alone in an empty house for the first time? How did he learn to ride a two-wheel bike? Who taught him to swim? What did his first kiss taste like? Who was his first real date? How did he feel when he passed his driver's license test? How did he talk some girl into having sex with him for the first time? What did his twenty-first birthday feel like? What was it like for him, holding his firstborn child in his arms? How did he take it, the first time he lost his job?

My Lady Wonder Wench has told me that her face in the mirror doesn't look at all like the face I see when she's lying on her pillow in the first light of dawn, slowly opening those soft blue eyes and turning the whole world the color of a Summer sky. That's the face I've seen for all these years, smiling and crying, and eating lobster on vacation, and cheering for the New York Mets. I know she has no idea how beautiful she is.

It's fascinating, looking carefully at your face in the mirror. It's like meeting somebody who knows you, but you can't quite remember him. I was thinking about that when we were walking in the park and we saw that old guy sitting on the bench just looking at the passing people. His eyes were wide open, but it was obvious that he was seeing a face the rest of us didn't know about. A face he'd seen waking up on the pillow next to him in the morning for a lot of years: smiling and crying, cheering for some baseball team, and now saving him a seat next to her—just like he asked her to do.

11-

Bark Stains On Your Collar

Big Louie likes his guys to be very careful about our romantic affairs. He says, for example, "There's nothing wrong with hugging a tree—as long as that's as far as it goes. You may have to back off a bit if your girlfriend or boyfriend finds bark stains on your shirt collar.

Another of his important bits of advice is, "Don't forget: relationships are between business people; lovers have romances. A relationship develops. A romance explodes."

Then there's Big Louie's equation for honesty in a romance; or actually it's about honesty in anything we've got going on. He says, "Honesty = The Truth + Maybe." That means whenever somebody says, "This is the truth; you've got to believe me," we should always think to ourselves, "Yeah? It's time for adding some, 'maybe."

As in, "It's perfectly obvious that the world is flat. Go look for yourself."

"We must go to war to keep the peace."

"UFO's? What... are you nuts?"

Big Louie says, "Always add that one word—maybe."

12-

Manly Fun and Games

I am stifling the screams of agony coming from some shocked muscles that thought they had retired several spring trainings ago, growing a new, thicker, and more tangled crop of chest hair, and reveling in the smell of sweat and gasoline that's stinking up the old jeans I'm wearing.

This afternoon was spent in a manly way felling trees with a chain saw and tossing huge logs into piles that stacked all the way to the roof—well, part of the way. Then, when I was sure my Lady Wonder Wench was watching out the window, I stalked all over the property with my shotgun for signs of bears or other predatory wildlife—which haven't actually been seen here since the James Madison administration—but my Lady was watching, so I figured I'd go stalking around anyway, just in case. All in all, it was an afternoon's work for some manly fun and games.

I love revving up that chain saw. Every time I do it, I know she's watching out the window.

And when I came in after felling the trees, clearing the property, and protecting her from saber-toothed squirrels, I noticed a little quiver in her voice when she said, "Oh my God, are you all right?"

My manly reply was, of course, a simple, "Of course, woman," spoken in my most resonant bass-baritone voice.

But I sometimes wonder if she's faking it. Because my friend Charles the Lawyer told me he called while I was out there being manly, and all she told him was "He's out in the yard."

I was out in the yard?

I was "out in the yard" is like saying the guy who won the Indy 500 was out driving around. "I was out in the yard"—right, like Tom Seaver was a baseball player. Like Donald Trump has hair. I was out in the yard.

As you guys know, it is sometimes difficult for a Louie Louie Generation guy to get his wife's attention. In a good way, I mean. In a manly way. I have often gotten my wife's attention in less positive ways. Like the Saturday morning last year when she noticed my college buddy Jerry coming down our driveway with his wife and five kids, and I realized I hadn't mentioned they were coming—for the weekend. I don't know why things like that sometimes slip my mind. Or when we were in an airliner at thirty thousand feet, going five hundred miles per hour on our way down to Florida to watch a week of spring training baseball a couple of years ago, and she asked me where I had put the tickets, and I suddenly remembered that they were still pinned to the bulletin board in the kitchen. That got her attention.

When I say some things, she has a very strange reaction. For example, for some reason anytime I say, "Watch this," she runs out of the room.

I'm a sexist. I like being manly. I can take my shirt off on a hot day. Nobody stops telling an off-color joke when I walk into a room. I can open applesauce jars. I get to look at my Lady W.W., and all she's got to look at is me. As far as I'm concerned, chocolate is just another snack. Manly.

I looked up the word "manly" in a thesaurus, and here's what it says the word means: audacious, bold, brave, confident, daring, dauntless, dignified, fearless, firm, gallant, hardy, heroic, hunk, muscular, noble, powerful, resolute, robust, self reliant, stately, strong, stud, vigorous, virile. Yes. I liked that. Especially that stud part. But then it added a word that blew it for me. Macho.

Macho is not manly. Macho is for wimps who are trying to impress the other guys. They are so afraid of the other guys that they strut and make a lot of noise and they don't do the number one thing a guy is supposed to do, which is to take care of women—and especially one woman. They'll tell you women can take care of themselves. And that's true. Some of these same words can apply to the best of women. Bold, brave, noble, resolute, self reliant, stately, strong ... but there's a word that macho guys always miss. It's a word that figures prominently in that document that the manly guys in the powdered wigs and funny hats wrote in Philadelphia all those years ago: "We pledge our lives, our fortunes, and our sacred honor ....." Our sacred honor. That's manly.

What an honor it is when a woman who can take care of herself, trusts a man enough to allow him to protect her. I guess one of the many fears that a macho guy must have is that he won't be up to the job. He won't be able to protect her. So he doesn't try. He's a wimp.

I didn't really cut down a lot of trees today. Just one, a little one. And the pile of wood was really only about enough for one long winter night's fire. And my Lady probably giggled about my stalking any stray saber-toothed squirrels with my shotgun.

But I like making her laugh, and that chain saw really does get her attention. Vroom, vroom. Manly. Bold, brave, noble, resolute, self reliant, stately and strong.

Manly.

overlooking an airport. So we scattered her ashes right over the beacon at our little home airport, New Garden Flying Field, just outside Philadelphia. And when we come home from a flight, we always say, "Hi, Mom. We're home. We still love you."

My Lady Wonder Wench and her mom, Helen, had an interesting relationship. Women's relationships are always more interesting than men's. We're easy. They're not. I think that's because, in some ways, they have to be tougher, and certainly smarter, than we do. I think when God created Adam, He took a look at what He'd done and figured He'd better create women, because it was pretty clear that we were going to need a lot of help.

So now you know the true story of Helen Hill. An unremarkable bump in the landscape, at a tiny, unremarkable airport, informally named for a woman who led a life that most people would call unremarkable. All Helen really did with her life was teach her kids to care about each other, to go to church, to work hard, and to be proud of being Americans.

That's all.

I think that's enough.

14-

The Funny Phone Fella

I just re-recorded the outgoing message on our phone machine. Louie Louie Generation guys like to think of ourselves as funny phone fellows. Our somewhat more evolved partners sometimes call us other names. They simply do not understand why we love weird outgoing phone machine messages. Most Louie Louie ladies are perfectly content to use the pre- recorded message that came with the machine, or they just say "You've reached the Smith residence. Please leave your name and phone number, and we'll get back to you as soon as we can." We, on the other hand, savor the opportunity. We have our callers by the ear, and they can't get away until we hit our punch line. This is our version of Jay Leno's monologue.

The short ones are the best. The one I just recorded says, "Hi. This is Dick. Please leave a message as soon as possible, and I'll get back to you at the sound of the beep." That replaced one that was too confusing I guess. It said, "Bridge. Kirk here. Beep me up, Scotty." You've got to be careful of doing something too confusing. I had one that said, "Hi. Dick's answering machine is broken. This is his refrigerator. Please speak very slowly, and I'll stick your message to my door with one of those little magnets." That got too many hang ups.

The one before that was "Hi, this is Dick. I'm sorry I can't answer the phone right now. Leave a message, and then wait by your phone until I call you back." I called myself a couple of times to hear that one, because it started all kinds of strange pictures going in my head.

Almost everybody has an answering machine these days. And be honest: don't you take advantage of that? Don't you sometimes call a guy you're really not anxious to talk to at the moment and hope you get his answering machine? That's soul satisfying. You've upheld your part of the staying-in-touch bargain without having to go through the agony of a lot of blah, blah, blah. Guys don't like a lot of blah, blah, blah. And after all, it's not your fault the guy wasn't there. The best time to do that is when you know he probably won't be around. Like when he's usually at work. But don't do that between midnight and dawn local time. The only time anybody's phone should ring in the middle of the night is when it's a wrong number.

Have you noticed that when somebody does call while you're asleep, you never admit you've been sleeping? You catch yourself saying things like "No, you didn't disturb me. Three in the morning? Really? I didn't notice. I was just kneeling in silent prayer, reading the Bible." But the worst time for the phone to ring is while you and your significant other are relating with each other significantly, and just as the earth is about to move, the phone rings. It's usually a recorded message trying to get you to vote for some idiot you never heard of, a spectacular once-in-a-lifetime vinyl-siding offer, or your chance to win an all-expenses-paid cruise to Siberia.

I've never understood why some guys really do stop moving the earth to answer a phone call. Any phone call. That has to be like going from highway speed right into reverse. Doesn't that sprain something semi-vital? And your romance is in really big trouble if you're in the middle of relating with your significant other, and all of a sudden you find yourself seriously considering making an outgoing call.

I like being the funny phone fella.

"Hello, this is you know who. We are you know where. Leave your you know what, you know when."

"Next on your classical request radio, we'll hear the music of Johan Sebastian Beep."

"Twinkle Twinkle little star, bet you're wondering where we are."

Betcha if Jay Leno recorded some of these, you'd laugh...a little.

15-

Dad Was a Guy

I'm sitting here in my big, manly, comfortable, black-leather poppa chair in the living room looking at a picture of my dad sitting in his big, comfortable, poppa chair in his living room a long time ago. He was the only hero I ever had. And that's too bad, because you don't really get to know the people who are your heroes. You know what they did. But you don't really know all the reasons why they did the things they did or how they felt about doing them.

We know that the first order George Washington gave his men when they crossed the Delaware that Christmas night in 1776 was "Burn the boats." My history book said that was so his men had no choice but to beat the Hessians at Trenton, because they had no boats to retreat to the other side of the river. But I wonder if he was also thinking, "Burning the damn boats will give these poor, freezing, barefoot, starving guys a few minutes of warmth before they go to lay down their lives for this thing we believe in."

We learn about Washington the hero—the gutsy, commanding guy who used his head and won our war. But I always wondered about Washington the man, the friend. How did he feel, watching his troops—a bunch of other guys, some of them his friends—on that frozen, awful night as they were getting ready to die to keep freedom warm and alive in their hearts and ours.

I wonder about Christ like that sometimes, too. Not the miracle worker, the supernatural Son of God, the second person of the Holy Trinity. I have kids, so I wonder about Christ as a baby, born in an animal's stable—the kid who must have been terrified by frequent nightmares of a cross and thorns and bloody nails. And how about the young man? He had disciples and followers. But was there some other guy he could trust to swap jokes with? And what was he feeling when a beautiful woman smiled at him? I wish I knew.

Dad was a teacher. Most heroes are. The things he taught were simple, yet profound. He said things like "There's a big difference between soft and gentle. It takes real strength to be gentle," and "There's a time for pulling yourself together, and there's a time for letting yourself go." He also said, "Be a man." And there wasn't any confusion about what he meant when he said that.

As a teacher, Dad knew that show was always more important than tell. So he showed me how to be a man. He always told the truth, even when he screwed up. So I never saw him get embarrassed, even when sometimes I saw him cry. He said, "Big boys never cry, but big men sometimes do." He loved to tell long, involved jokes to make me laugh. He liked laughing, especially when the joke was on him. He was deeply religious, in a very unusual way. He said, "The rules should be very strict, but the application of them should be very human, understanding, and loving." He was very smart. He was a whiz at math and music. Oh, he loved his music.

My room was right next to the living room where he had his piano. Most nights when I was a kid, he'd tell me a story, give me a kiss on the head, and go play his piano and sing in that quiet, gentle, powerful, baritone voice.

Dad wasn't a big guy. I'm taller than he was. But he kept himself strong. He was always doing push-ups. He was a college wrestler and a state champion quarter-mile track star. He was a peaceful guy, except if anybody gave my mom a hard time. I remember when I was a kid, that he came home one day and caught a delivery guy yelling at my mom. The delivery guy was a big, husky guy. Dad didn't say anything. He just picked the guy up and tossed him off the stoop. That was Dad's way of teaching me that job number one for any guy is taking care of your woman.

He was a hard worker. He taught music and ran a couple of church choirs. But he always found time to play catch with me and to teach me how to run a little faster and throw a pretty good punch. He also taught me how to play the saxophone—a little. I didn't have his talent. But my brother John did, and I was able to pass his talent down to three of my sons: David, Eric, and Mark. His wonderful way with numbers went to my son Kurt.

Dad also always took time to stop at the florist shop up the block to bring my mom a rose or two. Usually, he couldn't afford a dozen.

Dad had five sons. But he never had a daughter until my Lady Wonder Wench came into my life. When that happened, I had my Lady, and he had his daughter. The night he died, she leaned over and kissed his forehead. He opened his eyes and said, "That was very nice." I think those were his last words.

Mom had always wanted a daughter, too. And my Lady filled that need just as well as she did for Dad. My Lady became Mom's daughter, and her best friend.

A little while ago, I said I was almost sorry my dad was my hero—because I only saw what he did, and I never really found out why he did those things. I think that's a guy thing. And it's too bad. I don't think I ever knew Dad very well as just a guy—a guy with a wife and five kids and a mortgage and aches and pains and hopes and fears. I never had the slightest idea about his hopes and fears. Especially his fears. He must have had some. I think my Lady

Wonder Wench got to know him better than I ever did. She knew him well enough to be the daughter he always wanted. She was never his "daughter in law." She was the daughter he always wanted, and maybe needed.

I think the reason why guys always hope to have a daughter is that we'd kind of like to have someone who's smart enough and caring enough to find out not just what we do, but why we do it—and how we feel about what we've done. I'll never forget the day our daughter Kris was born. She opened her eyes, looked up at me, squinted a little, gave a little half smile that said "Hi, I know who you are. I'll be your daughter, so don't worry about a thing," and went back to sleep. From that day on, I always tried to be the kind of guy she thinks I am. I don't always make it. But I always try.

I'm looking at Dad's picture on the wall right now, and let me tell you, I'm taller than he was, but I have a lot of growing to do to come close to being anywhere near his size.

16-

Dog Gone

I'm watching my Lady Wonder Wench sitting on the couch across the room. She is pretending that she doesn't notice that I'm watching her, because I am in the doghouse. Actually, it's because I'm not in a doghouse. There is no dog in this house, and my Lady has been hinting that we should fix what she calls "that problem." I don't see that as a problem—and by hinting, I mean she has been saying things like "Why don't we get a dog?"

Now, I realize that what I am about to say will put me high up on any decent person's list of surly, soulless, scoundrels. But I don't want a dog in my life right now. I also realize that it's statements like that cause a great many—mostly unnecessary—fatal fights between men and women. And I understand that one of the things she's thinking now is "If I throw a stick, will he run after it—and just keep running?"

My buddy Jerry and his wife Doris have a dog, which they treat like their child. My feeling is that I have had enough children. And besides, I fear that the mixing of human and dog DNA could well result in the creation of an animal which, instead of barking, would look up at you and say, "Let my people go."

Dogs are smart. I think some of them can count. I remember how snotty my dog Whistle got one day when I put three dog biscuits in my pocket and fed him only two of them. Whistle was the family mutt while I was growing up. I realize now that a dog is an almost equal partner with the rest of the family in raising a kid. I learned a lot from Whistle: obedience, loyalty, and the need to turn around three times before lying down.

Please don't misunderstand. I like dogs. I just don't like dog poop, dog hair, and the dog-gone hassle of taking walks in the snow looking for fire hydrants and trees. I am not really a terrible person for not wanting a dog in my life right now. I may be a terrible person, but not for that reason. I've just been a highly responsible guy all my life. And now, four out of the five voices in my head are telling me it's time I let the little kid inside me out to play. Just me and my Lady W.W.

I want to take her for dinner at the kind of restaurant where she gets to wear that slinky black dress with the sheer sleeves in the candlelight. Or jump in our little airplane and go flying on a clear night that's full of a full moon. I want to go necking with her at every opportunity, including long stoplights. I do not want a dog's nose intruding itself into moments like that.

I have nothing against dogs or any other animal. I am an animal myself, come to think of it. But we've had dogs—and kids—and you've got to treat dogs and kids responsibly. We have a little time left, my Lady and me, and I'd like to spend it with just her. But she's looking at me like, Let's talk this over like a couple of responsible adults. No, I have tried to pretend I'm a responsible adult all my life.

I have to be careful here, because I know there are things husbands and wives have to be careful about saying to each other in tricky situations like this. And I hope my Lady Wonder Wench pays attention to what Big Louie says about that: "There are two words that, more than any other words, make life awful for men in situations like this. The two words women should never say to their guys are, 'Don't' and 'Stop.' You women should never say those words 'Don't' and 'Stop' to any guy with whom you are in a committed romantic relationship—unless those words are used together with no space in between."

I can't help it. Right now, I want to be the only animal in my Lady Wonder Wench's life.

And I know how to deal with this.

Goldfish.

17-

Jelly Beans, Daffodils, and Bedtime Stories

I'm feeling a little choked up. My Lady Wonder Wench wrote a comment in her blog Wednesday about the fact that I forgot our wedding anniversary again. But instead of complaining that the census had the nerve to list me as a human being this year she said, "My Louie Louie lad remembers me all the time with jelly beans, daffodils, holding hands, laughing at silly jokes, and bedtime stories. Don't get me wrong, I love getting jewelry and candy and flowers and fancy dinners and marvelous blouses from very fancy shops. But I love my Louie Louie lad more."

That's the kind of thing that will make a Louie Louie guy like me stand up very straight, look her right in the eyes, and kiss her face until my fillings melt. She slips sexy notes into my shirt pockets. She plays with me and laughs. She makes me feel powerful, because she lets me make her feel beautiful. I am some kind of lucky guy.

I know a couple of you are having your hearts wrung out right now. And that's the kind of thing that can make you begin to believe that nothing you always knew about somebody—and counted on—was real. You can begin to question whether the things you did together ever really happened. You can even begin to think that you'll never let yourself feel anything again; in fact, you can't remember ever feeling anything.

I don't tell you about how good it is with my Lady to hurt you. I tell you about it because you know we've been together for a very long time, and I want you to know this kind of romance really does happen. Sometimes it does work. I don't know for sure if it will ever work for you, but I also know, that you don't know either…for sure… that it won't.

I like Big Louie's simple advice: "We've got to stop snarling when we talk to ourselves." It's true. We're always talking about things that go wrong. It's like some tiny Darth-Vader-Dreadful-Drone is lurking in our heads, whispering, "Come over to the dork side. We've got cookies."

I've had about enough of the dork side. Tune in to any news channel and about the most optimistic thing you hear is that "things aren't getting worse quite as fast as they were yesterday. So have as nice a day as you can under the circumstances."

There are lots of fun, happy, sometimes silly things going on around us all the time. There's a sign in front of the hardware store down the street that was supposed to say something about a special on screws, but today it's saying something the guy who put it there certainly didn't intend it to say because one of the letters fell off. How about the feeling you get when you slip a silk handkerchief in your jacket pocket? And I love to put a smile on the face of the waitress in the Japanese restaurant where we like to have sushi when I remember how to say "Domo arigato." And just now I was listening to my Lady Wonder Wench laughing while she was snapping the bubbles in a long strip of bubble wrap.

It made me remember her standing there in my office—a long time ago—saying, "I'm here for the secretarial job." She was wearing a soft gray sweater and a plaid skirt with pleats that made it flare a little. When she took a step, the hem hesitated a little until it moved to catch up with her hips. She said, "I'm here about the secretarial job," but I was hearing, "I'm here because I'm supposed to be your girlfriend."

She really was my first girlfriend. The first female person in my life who actually wanted me to get to know her. To see her. And then to touch her. And to bring her jelly beans and daffodils and hold her hand and laugh together at silly jokes and tell each other long—now decades long—bedtime stories.

And if your heart is being wrung out right now, I want you to know that sometimes, very old bedtime stories really do have very long, happy endings.

18-

Coming Out of the Closet

Let me be very clear about what I mean when I say I'm coming out of the closet. I've been looking at the bulging door of the office closet where I keep my stuff. I didn't expect to find a treasure that I haven't seen since 1982 in there, because it's just my stuff closet. You know—my stuff. My reel-to-reel tape recorder, my back issues of Time magazine, my living room lava lamps... you've probably got a closet full of stuff like that too. And I figured that since I can't finish the job I was planning on doing, cutting the grass, I might as well take on the battle of the bulge—the bulge in the door.

The grass situation is a little out of control. Actually it's mostly weeds, according to my Lady Wonder Wench and other botanical experts, but it's green, it grows, and it looks okay if you keep it cut. But I've been busy working, so I have left it somewhat uncut. My Lady Wonder Wench has been suggesting that the onrushing weeds are so high that they're beginning to cut off the view of our driveway from our living room window. My perfectly reasoned and completely masculine response—that I don't particularly miss seeing our driveway—doesn't seem to have been completely satisfactory to her. It is true that I certainly don't want any of the large, hairy beasts that she claims may have moved into the lawn under cover of darkness last night to carry her off to some grassy cave so they can have their way with her. And I hate it when our mail guy, Bill, whines about having to reach through the weeds to open our mailbox.

So, it was past time for me to put on my lawn-tractor man T-shirt and go on the attack. But I can't lawn tractor around some of the lawn. It's not that I'm afraid of getting swallowed up by the taller weeds or being attacked by big, sneaky, hairy creatures. There are just some very rocky, and very hilly places where I've just got to resort to weed whacking and push mower-ing. So I did. And right in the middle of my push mower-ing, my Louie Louie left leg attacked me.

As Big Louie has often explained, there are terrific benefits to being a Louie Louie Generation guy. But there are also some problems. And I immediately knew it was problem time when I heard a distinct "sprong" from under my left knee cap, the muscle on my left hip jumped up and hid in my left armpit, and for a moment I saw and heard the New York Fourth of July fireworks display going off in my head. Somehow, in an instant, I became a quivering bucket of powerless, Louie-Louie Generation heavy-breathing molecules.

I don't like that. Being powerless sucks. I have very seldom felt powerless in my lifetime. Think about it. Lois Lane loved Superman, but she didn't even see Clark Kent. He was a nice guy—smart, vulnerable, honest, good job, but powerless. She didn't want a powerless nice guy, even when he's smart, vulnerable and honest. And I don't blame her. I believe that the difference between living and just existing is in your power. Your power can be physical, emotional, spiritual, financial, or whatever kind of power that works for you. And maybe most of all, I believe in the awesome power of your personal beliefs.

I believe in a lot of things. I believe it's a terrible waste to let ourselves turn into warm chunks of meat just because we don't look like the people in the beer commercials any more with their fancy-shmancy abs and perky breasts. I believe in honesty, truth, motherhood, baseball, and highway safety. I believe justice should be enforced with compassion. I believe in the American Dream… whatever that is…uniquely and individually…for each and every one of us. My God think of the power in that. I believe in Santa Claus, and in loving the same woman for a lot of years…and for as many years as we may be lucky enough to have left… I believe real men don't care if people see them cry. I believe men and women are supposed to be different. I believe in magic, and wooden baseball bats; I love the way they feel, and the sound they make smacking the ball; and I believe in the healing power of chicken soup and peanut butter- the chunky kind, and keeping your hormones humming, and laughing at yourself, and the worthlessness of guilt, excuses, and gangsta rap, and the tingle inside when you take a deep breath of very fresh air, and letting go of your kids when it's time…that's hard… and taking care of your mom when your dad dies, and working your ass off, and maybe most of all I believe in being grateful for what you've got. Really grateful. That's the attitude/gratitude connection. I believe that if you stay grateful and happy, it'll help keep you healthy, and when you're feeling healthy, you're still hot…no matter what the calendar says. What do you believe ?

I haven't seen the treasure I found in that closet since 1982. The magic in that treasure made the sprong in the kneecap, the hip muscle hiding under my arm pit, and the fireworks in the head all go away.

Sometimes the biggest treasure gets packed into the littlest package. And so it was with this small, yellowed, clipping from a 1982 Cleveland newspaper. It says, and I quote, "Eleven-year-old Amy Burnett of Burton placed first in the recent Rainbow Babies and Children's Hospital art contest. She received a five-dollar gift certificate for ice cream. Her design was picked from among sixty received and was printed on 74,000 greeting cards to be used to raise money for the hospital. 'Hasn't this been an exciting day,' Amy murmured to her mother after the choice was announced. She died an hour later of cystic fibrosis, which she had suffered from since she was three."

Hasn't this been an exciting day.

I don't know how a loving power in charge of the universe could let an innocent little kid suffer and die like that. I believe in love, and I couldn't find any there. But as I was looking, I did find something...absolutely Godly.

"Hasn't this been an exciting day," she said. The Master of the universe cut her life cruelly short. But in her last hour, He let her win...just that once. It's an awesome lesson. He gave her the priceless treasure of "such an exciting day" to take with her into eternity. Such a priceless treasure, and such a lesson to us, given in just that one moment of simple, complete, loving...compassion.

19-

Auto-Cannibalism

I was enjoying dinner with my Lady Wonder Wench this evening, when I had a sudden and painful attack of auto-cannibalism. For those of you who are not medical experts, auto-cannibalism has nothing to do with eating your car. And since it's a condition that happens almost exclusively to Louie Louie Generation guys, Big Louie would want me to tell you about it right away.

Auto-cannibalism is the condition that makes you bite your own tongue. Why do we do that? I have a theory: Don't blame it on your eye teeth—that would be funny but inaccurate. We frequently strive for inaccuracy here but not this time. As you very well know, your eye teeth can't actually see anything.

That does bring into question the current practice of putting a blue tooth in your ear so you can hear phone conversations. That's a really weird picture, which we may develop at a later time.

But back to my auto-cannibalism theory; I think it happens mostly to Louie-Louie Generation guys, because unlike women, our tongues get fat. Looking around, I have noticed that lots of Louie Louie lads have allowed many parts of our bodies to get fat. Especially parts like our heads, which as you know, is where most of us keep our tongues. And fat tongues are easy targets for fast moving teeth.

For those of you who are not Louie Louie Generation guys and therefore don't have this problem, let me explain what it's like when auto-cannibalism strikes: All of a sudden your fingers stiffen and then in one powerful spasm, they fold backwards—almost all the way back so your nails touch your knuckles—and very naughty words grind out between your clenched teeth, and your eyes bulge out like mine did last Saturday when I realized I had left my wallet with my credit cards, my pay check, and all my personal IDs back at the supermarket checkout, and the supermarket was by then a very, very, very, very long way back in my rearview mirror.

There is no pain that compares with auto-cannibalism. As I said, it's a condition that almost exclusively attacks Louie Louie Generation guys. I'm glad women don't usually suffer from auto-cannibalism. But if they did, they would no longer complain about the relatively insignificant pain of childbirth. The only comparable pain known to doctors who have gone to actual (as opposed to Internet) medical schools, is the pain, which is also experienced only by guys, and that is the pain that comes from putting your arm around the back of your wife's or girlfriend's chair at the movies and leaving it there for two and a half hours. And then, she likes the movie so much that she wants to stay and watch all the closing credits: best boy, grip, the whole thing.

My Lady Wonder Wench has a theory about the reason Louie Louie Generation guys' tongues grow that fat. She says it's simple: we don't exercise our tongues by having long conversations about relationships with those with whom we share a romance. Lady Wonder Wench is very smart, so I think there may be some merit to that idea.

But then, isn't the opposite also true? Doesn't it make sense that ladies' tongues grow slim, shapely, and muscular because they have the benefit of years of heavy-duty, nonstop, aerobic exercise in the discussion of similar topics? Whatever theory you buy, the result is obvious, and I guess we have to simply put it down as one more example of the differences between men and women.

I really do think that women in general have much more control over their bodies than we do. For example, I even have runaway eyebrows. When my Lady W. W. walks into the room wearing something she calls "a little more comfortable" or when she comes over, looks up at me and just smiles that slow smile, and gives me a long lovely kiss, my eyebrows twitch and my ears wiggle. I can't help it. Just thinking about it right now, my ears are creating a small breeze up there on my forehead. I will leave for your own consideration a list of some other bodily parts over which men have very little control. No wonder why we're always trying to figure out what part of us is going to wear out first. Not a good thing.

But lots of good things did happen to me this week: I folded up a road map exactly the way I found it. My Lady Wonder Wench put a bouquet of fresh tulips on our dinner table, and we lit two tall slim candles to go with them. Beautiful. She was exercising her hurt hand with some silly putty, so we had a little game of catch with it when she was finished. I made a paper airplane that had a graceful flight from the kitchen all the way to the living room wall. I found the name "Robert Marshall" written in old fashioned handwriting and faded ink, on the inside cover of an old book in a second hand book store, and I started making up an imaginary bigography for him. The wind the other day blew the tarp off my snow blower. My neighbor Randy found it in his yard, and he came over last night and put it back on. And my brother John, his wife Beth, our son Mark and his Lady Donna, our Tall Guy son Eric and his wife Brenda, came to visit for my birthday … and we told terrible knock-knock jokes and puns … late into the night. And we laughed till we started to cry … and then we started to laugh again.

Lots of little good things happened this week. The kind of stuff that can almost make up for all the pain of the big bad stuff that's going on in the world these days. Almost all that pain can be overcome.

All but the pain caused by auto-cannibalism. Ooo, that hurts.

20-

Sister Mary Knucklebuster

Having nothing better to fondle at the moment, I am fondling some fond memories. I remember standing in front of a classroom packed with my peers, confessing to worshiping false Gods, disrespecting my parents, and murder, when suddenly, the word "Richard" rang out loud and clear in the unmistakable voice of my first communion teacher, Sister Mary Knucklebuster. Sister Knucklebuster represented the Roman Catholic Church at St. Gregory's grammar school in Brooklyn in much the same way that General George Patton represented the United States Army. She was tall, stern, and tough. And she was presiding over my class's rehearsal for first confession. It was my turn to stand in front of the room and recite the famous formula, "Bless me, Father, for I have sinned."

Please get the picture: I was seven years old, and Sister suddenly realized that in order to come up with material to confess, I was going down the Moses top-ten no-no list. That means after confessing to murder, which is number five, I was about to confess to adultery and coveting my neighbor's wife.

But just in the nick of time, her voice exploded from somewhere deep down in that Darth Vader veil.

"Richard," she said, "that will do. Just say your sin was disobeying your parents."

So that's what I said in the rehearsal—and in all subsequent confessions right up through high school—my reasoning being that whatever sin the devil might have made me commit with Jeanie or Matilda or Maureen, my parents would have said I shouldn't do that. So I really was disobeying my parents when I went surfing on my newly discovered testosterone tsunamis into forbidden hormonal happiness.

Richard was my dad's name. It's a perfectly respectable name. But I prefer being called Dick for many reasons, not the least of which is that I get a kick out of watching some folks blush. Somehow, D, as in Dick, has become the new N word, to some of the more uptight members of the Politically Correct Forces for Good in the Community, because they can't get over one of the slang meanings of my name. I suspect that some of those people spend way too much of their spare time sitting in closets, pulling wings off flies, fondling their Jello, and drooling over old National Geographic magazines.

When I hear somebody call me Richard, I know I'm probably in trouble. I am Richard on my pilot's license and my driver's license, but Dick on my credit card. That has caused ID problems at major airports, most recently at Philadelphia International, when the Pimple Person Princess doing the screening wouldn't believe that Dick is a nickname for Richard. I reminded her that former Vice President Richard Cheney is often called Dick. But in typical Pimple Person fashion, she asked, "Who is Dick Cheney?"

My Lady Wonder Wench who, like many Louie Louie ladies, is more deeply concerned with remaining inside the limits of good taste than I am, calls me "Richard" when, like most Louie Louie Generation guys, I occasionally try sneaking under one of those limits of good taste ... like when I pick my teeth at the table ... or unavoidably emit some personal sound and fragrance. She at one time had a rather observant parrot who picked up on the idea that anything nasty was a "Richard." Therefore, he called anything that displeased him a "Richard." I caught him one day sitting in his cage, spitting at our daughter's kitten and calling him a "Richard."

The reason I'm fondling these memories it that a Saint Gregory's alumni magazine came in today's mail. There was a picture of Sister Mary Knucklebuster on the obituary page. I almost didn't recognize her. That wasn't her real name, of course it was just a nasty name a bunch of snotty kids called her behind her back a long time ago. The name under the picture wasn't her real name either. Nuns' real names are taken from them, along with everything they own when they join the convent. I started to wonder: who were you, really, Sister Mary Knucklebuster?

Whoever you were, it's way past time for me to say thank you for all the fond memories I have of those days. So, thank you, whoever you were. And as a matter of fact, on behalf of so many guys who were snotty 7 year old kids in so many of the classrooms you faced for so many years; thank you for your life.

21-

We're Only Guys

Many people of all generations who are not guys will sometimes call those of us who are Louie Louie Generation guys "Maturity Challenged." And they're right. But it's not our fault. The "Big Louie Institute for Fooling Around and Figuring Most Things Out" released a report recently that explains the whole thing.

The report notes that a guy's brain is swimming in a sea of testosterone, which gives him a deep voice, a beard, and a hand just the right size for using a TV remote. The testosterone in which his brain swims also absorbs some of the shocks of life that sometimes hit him right in the head. Like a baseball, an unexpected blast of Yanni's music, or high levels of verbal communication.

Now please remember, testosterone is a preservative. And what does a preservative do? It keeps meat and stuff from growing old and gnarly. And, of course, growing is another word for maturing. So naturally, a brain swimming in testosterone simply cannot grow and mature.

It's not our fault. We're only guys. We do the best we can with what we have to work with.

22-

The R Word

I'm sitting here in my big, comfortable, black leather pappa chair in my living room, in total shock. My Lady Wonder Wench just said the R word. I think I'd better stand up for a moment, just to prove I still can. There. That's better. I knew I could do it. I know that as a true Louie Louie Generation gentleman, my years of having young lovelies whispering the word "hunk" behind my back in lustful awe may well be way back in my rear view mirror. Come to think about it, there are now young lovelies…and not so young ones… cruel ones all…who might possibly say my rear simply isn't really worth viewing at all anymore. It's times like these when it's important to remember what Big Louie, his own bad self, the Chief Mustard Cutter of the Louie-Louie Generation always says: "You can only hold your belly in for so many years."

She said the R word to me. Me. The former chief lifeguard at Coney Island's section 6. A guy who had his own TV Bandstand show. A manly man who proudly wore his speedo bathing suit since high school until it mysteriously disappeared a few years ago. (You know… I now suspect that she might have had something to do with that disappearance.) She said the R word…to me.

I do have to lose a few pounds. And that's no walk in the park. Come to think of it no walk in the park is probably part of the reason I have to lose a few pounds. I still make my hand prints in the carpet doing my push-ups, and I huff and puff around the neighborhood on my bike, because I really don't want my body to attack me. And I have now officially become a glasses guy...I have to wear them all the time now. You get used to it. In fact, I realized while I was doing my pushups today that I was still wearing my glasses. That was weird.

Former gym teachers who now call themselves personal trainers so they can charge $100 an hour, try to make figuring out your physical condition complicated. It's not complicated. It's simple. If it jiggles, it's fat. Of course, remember that fat is not always bad. As I'm sure you have observed, it depends on where it is. "Fat" looks quite nice on the upper bodies of some ladies of my acquaintance for example.

But this is not about my somewhat rusting physical condition. It's about the R word. She said it to me today. She said, "Why don't you retire." When I got control of my eyebrows and my tongue, I tried giving her a respectful and typically male, perfectly reasoned answer. I said "I've had an easy life. I was a disc jockey and a therapist. I'm not tired. Think of the word "re-tire." It means you've got to tire first, and then get peppy again before you can re-tire. I've been running around having fun all my life. How am I going to all of a sudden learn to do nothing and then rest ?" That's pretty well reasoned isn't it ?

I like what I do. It's not much but I like it, and the pay is decent. I do the communications for a very successful law firm...I make their commercials and I write their newsletter...stuff like that. I've known the guys who own the company for years, and they're good guys. They treat me with respect, and they do the kind of work anybody would be proud to represent. So why should I retire ? I'm really only thirty...inside. That's where it counts.

Right ?

I'll have to admit that I have been snarling a bit lately towards the end of the week. And I'm going to have to run out to the west coast again next week. And when I get really busy, My Lady Wonder Wench starts looking a little lonesome, sitting on the couch doing her needlepoint. I don't like it when Lady Wonder Wench isn't happy. She put the 'tude in my life.. She has taken care of the kids, and the house, and me…for a long time. This idea of retiring sneaks up on you like a windshield sneaks up on the backside of a bug on a summer night. I bet inside every retired person there's some kid who's just starting out…looking around and saying…"hey, what happened."

It seems like just when you begin to get a handle on the way things really are, the handle falls off. Louie Louie Generation folks have learned some important lessons, like, whether the glass is half full or half empty mostly depends on whether you're drinking or pouring. And there is no such thing as safe sex. And if you walk around looking like you know what you're doing, you can usually get away with doing anything you want to do…except fly an airplane, perform brain surgery, or do your own income tax. And when you're thinking of buying a used car, check the station buttons on the radio. If they're all set to rock stations, chances are the transmission is shot. .

I know. It's all part of growing up. You've got to learn you'll get into trouble if you go up to the check out counter at the drug store with a box of condoms, and ask the manager "Where's the fitting room."

I was only kidding, but the guy had no sense of humor.

How can a maturity challenged Louie-Louie Generation guy like me even think about retiring ? Retire. Me?

You know what ? The idea scares the hell out of me.

72

23-

Shower Power

I'm sitting here in my big, comfortable, black-leather poppa chair, after a really tough day. Just popped off the shoes. Don't know if I should put these socks in the laundry or set fire to them. It probably doesn't matter because they might set off the fire alarm without any help from a match either way. I'm really looking forward to taking a nice, hot shower in a few minutes. It's been a tough day but a good day. I got stuff done. Getting things done feels good. It makes you feel like you're in control, and there's not a lot of that in-control feeling around these days. That's why we've got burnout.

Out on the road, you've got to compete with people driving at speeds ranging from sonic boom to car wash—and all you want to do is get to work. You've got to be cunning to survive. Of course, Big Louie, his own bad self, has some advice for surviving in today's traffic. For example, Louie says, "Never pass a driver who's on a cell phone. Neither that driver nor you have any control in that situation. Wait till he creams the truck ahead of him, then pass briskly on whichever side has less debris."

Most of our lives seem like they're out of our control. It started for me when Dad confiscated my comic books because Mom said

I was spending too much time checking out Wonder Woman. I sometimes wonder what he did with them.

When I started dating, my first potential co-necker fell asleep in the backseat of the car. Just as well I guess, we'd probably have gotten our braces locked together. I drove into a McDonald's for a cup of coffee the other day, and the lid of the coffee cup said something to the effect of, "For God's sake, don't spill this stuff on your lap anywhere near a zip code that might contain a lawyer." It's my coffee. I should be able to spill it anywhere I like.

Life is out of our control. That's where we get burnout. And I'm not kidding about that. Working hard doesn't burn you out. Burn out isn't in your muscles. It's in your head. And we're passing it onto our kids. We should stop that.

"Eat every pea on your plate or no dessert."

"Bang that glass one more time and I'll sell you."

"No singing at the table."

"Shut your mouth and eat."

We need eating-dinner songs. Singing would take your mind off the fact that peas will kill you.

The Original Designer of Genes didn't plan things this way. He made guys like Tarzan. Tarzan could, and did, sing and holler all he wanted when he ate. He never ate peas. Only lions. And not only did he get dessert, Jane served it to him. Not sure what was in it for Jane.

Where did we go wrong? If some guy tried to stop some other guy from singing around the ol' cave campfire, Pow! He got a fast face full of fossil fist. If some nasty Neanderthal tried to make a cave lady eat peas, she just said, "Buzz off, buster, and come back when you've evolved a little further."

Now, if an unexpected visitor wearing a mask climbs into your bedroom window at 3:00 A.M., you don't call a cop—you call your lawyer. And do you know what your lawyer will say? "Don't hurt him. He'll sue. Give him the benefit of the doubt. Maybe he's lost. Discuss his disadvantaged youth with him. If he's bouncing something that looks suspiciously like a policeman rolled up into a ball, encourage him to join the other youths at the playground for a game of basketball. Tell him he looks like the Lone Ranger in that mask. Say, 'Have a nice day.'"

Not only are we not allowed to sing at the table, we're not even allowed to peek under that guy's mask. Burnout feels like it sounds. Like there's a patch of slick ice, and you're a giant tire spinning and smoking, skidding around and slamming into things, getting hurt. You're out of control.

My Lady Wonder Wench put my burnout out a long time ago. She just said, "Do whatever you want to do. You can do it." And she meant it. And now what I most want to do is to take that long, hot shower—with her. It's my shower. I should be able to take it any way I want. Right?

24-

Light Up Your Limbics

I'm trying to come to grips with the fact that, once again, I was passed over in the selection of the sexiest man in the world by People magazine, which is probably the most popular magazine currently published by the Pimple People Press. You know how certain talking heads broadcasters always slam the main stream media? Now as you know, Louie Louie Generation gentlemen can't be bothered slamming anybody, but we do know how to put things into perspective. So let's put the Pimple People Press into perspective. In fact, let's put the Pimple People into perspective

This is now several years in a row that I have missed being voted the sexiest man in the world. But generally, I'm handling the disappointment well I think. Because I know my limbics are in good shape, and theirs aren't. As you know your limbic system is the part of your brain that makes you go "EEE-HAA." It therefore is the part that most often gets you into trouble. So, like most Louie-Louie Generation guys, I understand and sympathize with the shallow thinking and questionable taste that are the trademarks of the Pimple People in general. They simply don't have our experience, our charm, our understanding of worldly affairs. And it's not their fault. They're kids ! They don't have a clue. They've probably never even heard our theme song, "Louie Louie." We take control, and boost our sexiness levels simply by humming it to ourselves. Then we smile, and they have no idea what we're thinking about that's making us smile.

Some Pimple People guys don't mind sharing their girlfriends and wives with their buddies. And the Pimple Princesses don't seem to mind that. I don't understand them any better than they probably understand me.

So, as a public service, I thought I'd give the members of the Pimple People a list of what's really sexy to one Louie-Louie Generation guy: me. Nobody can speak for all Louie Louie Generation guys, because our tastes are so rich and varied. But here is the countdown of the top ten turn-ons for me.

10. The dance. George Harrison said it: "There's something in the way she moves." My Lady Wonder Wench will sometimes stretch, swivel her hips, smile, and sit down slowly. It's like watching raw silk unfold. I'll bet fashion models practice moving like that in front of a mirror. It makes my eyebrows twitch and my ears wiggle, and it often causes other even more basic physical reactions.

9. Her arm in a sleeveless summer blouse. It makes me want to kiss her all the way up to where the blouse begins at the tip of her shoulder. That makes her tilt her head to that side and smile. She knows I don't want to stop kissing her there. I think she turns her head a little because she's a little ticklish in certain feminine places. She smiles because her limbic system lights up too.

8. I love touching her. Not just in sexy places. Actually, almost any place can be sexy. I love touching her face or the smooth back of her neck, lying on a pillow in the first light of dawn filtering through our bedroom window...

7. Has to be her eyes. Especially when they're sparkling and laughing because she's with me. I love looking into her eyes for a

long, long time. They get very big and very blue, and then sometimes they close very slowly.

6. She has a sultry voice. Soft, and smiling, and low. It comes from all the way inside her. It makes me want to know all of the most delicious thoughts that are making her laughs so smooth and sexy. I love the sound of that voice saying things only I am ever going to hear.

5. Walking into an empty bedroom and catching the last wisp of her perfume. It makes me wonder…and fantasize that the fragrance was all she was wearing. And I wonder what she's wearing now. So much of sexiness is in the wondering. Wondering is what you do when you're in the presence of magic. Not card tricks. Magic.

4. Her scent. I love her smell. Including her sweat. I love the look, the scent, and the feel of her sweat. It's the opposite of "kool." I don't care for kool. I love hot.

3. Sharing a shower or a hot tub. Warm water washes away a lot of years and aches and pains. It takes me back to my days as a young beach lifeguard at Coney Island. It really was even better than Baywatch showed you: in the waves; on the hot sand; and under the boardwalk. I didn't know my Lady Wonder Wench then. Sharing a shower or a hot tub helps me time-travel back all those years—but this time, with her.

2. I don't think I'll tell you about number two. I'll just sit here and enjoy thinking about it. You're very welcome to join me by sitting there and thinking about your own number two.

1. My Lady is a fanatic New York Mets baseball fan. So I sometimes call her my Baseball Babe. And she has some of the most dangerous curves known to mankind. She makes my limbic system light up enough to play an all-night game, just by pitching me any one of those curves. The poor Pimple People just wouldn't understand. And the Dreary Drones fell asleep long ago.

25-

Speed Bumps

C arly Simon was singing, "These are the good old days," on my car's CD player when I hit a speed bump driving home from the supermarket today. The CD skipped, lots of groceries bounced around in the trunk, and the little jonquil plant I bought for my Lady Wonder Wench left a dirty little comment on the backseat. Fortunately for me, all the world loves a four-letter word.

I first heard that song while I was doing the morning show at WPLJ Radio in New York. I like Carly, and I got to do a special with her for the old Westwood One radio network. That was fun. But I remember thinking when I first heard her sing that song in 1972, You've got to be kidding, Carly. We had the Vietnam War and Watergate, eleven Israeli athletes were murdered in the Munich Olympics, and only 55 percent of Americans bothered to vote—and they elected Richard Nixon. I remember thinking, these are the good old days? I don't think so. But looking back at what we've got going on right now, maybe she was right.

And maybe these are, too—the good old days, I mean. As Big Louie always says, "There are makers, there are takers, and there are fakers." And it sure seems like the takers and the fakers have turned what we're doing with the world into something that looks like a million-times-magnified cold virus.

But I got to thinking, what if the seventies really were the good old days then, and these are the good old days now, and we just aren't paying attention? We're too busy complaining. We do that kind of thing. We spend the first half of our lives complaining about our parents, and the second half of our lives complaining about our kids and grandkids.

It's easy to find stuff to complain about. It's all over TV, radio, and what's left of the newspapers. Nasty stuff is always big news. "If it bleeds, it leads." Negative stuff always gets our attention. The fact of the matter is that we love to complain because it's always easier to complain than it is to create. Film critics are a dime a dozen, but there's only one Steven Spielberg. When I was a therapist, I always asked people what they wanted in their lives. They always told me what they didn't want, instead.

"I don't want to be fat anymore."

"I don't want to have my heart broken any more."

"I don't want to remember my terrible childhood anymore."

Fifty years old and some guy is complaining about being toilet trained at gunpoint. Time to hit a speed bump, fella. Time to stop sucking your thumb and use it to hitch a ride to someplace better in your life. Time to double 'tude. Get happy, healthy and hot.

I'm a lucky guy. I've got my Lady Wonder Wench, a nice home, a good job that I like, and a couple of real friends; I even have my own little airplane, red bulbs in my bedroom, and most of my family is still talking to me. I have red light bulbs in my bedroom because red bulbs are the Big Louie-approved wrinkle erasers. They make you look like yourself, only younger. You put some red light bulbs around in strategic places, and as long as you still have some moveable parts, you're okay.

Speed bumps are only a couple of inches high. But they get your attention. They make you slow down, look around, and notice that you've been taking corners on two wheels. Maybe we've been paying too much attention to the guys on TV who are making millions by singing that old song that goes "We're in danger, there's no doubt, so run in circles, scream and shout." I like Carly's song better.

Lots of stuff that's going on right now can make you feel like you're the Pillsbury Doughboy meeting a vehicle operated by Joe's Asphalt and Concrete Paving Company. It can make you want to run.

But, as Big Louie says, "Remember the speed bumps." He means the little things that deserve your attention: A very soft carpet under your toes. A sweet pine fire. Sunlight on your shoulders. A pair of really sharp sunglasses. A bubble-gum-bubble the size of your fist. A good back scratch. An absolutely still, star-studded, clear, winter night. The sounds a baby makes trying to say "Mommy." The words, "Once upon a time" in an old familiar voice. Pitchers and catchers reporting for spring training. Having dinner with someone lovely in a restaurant built in a tiny old house with slanted floors and a real fireplace. Sunday-mornin-church bells ringing in the steeple of a newly painted white, New England village church. Soft, warm skin in tempting red velvet.

We can't change what is. But we can change what we think about what is, and what we do about it. Speed bumps. Stop and smell the jonquils. I saved them from the back seat, and right now I'm sitting here watching them open in the little pot on our kitchen table.

Maybe Carly was right.

26-

Tummy Tux

Once upon a time, a long, long time ago when I was twelve, I had a friend by the name of Eddie Kelly, who lived across the street. He was thirteen, so he knew all about girls. He said, "Girls like guys with big muscles." So I started doing push-ups. Big time. I figured I wouldn't have to be just another sock in the Laundromat of life; if I had big muscles, I could be a serious chick magnet. But as my muscles grew, so did my realization that many of the girls who were the most attracted to muscle magnets were the kind of girls who often forgot to bathe. I think some of them were attracted to muscle magnets because they may have had had steel teeth.

I got heavily into doing pushups, even though I hated doing them. Everybody does. You never see a guy doing push-ups with a smile on his face. But I've been at it since I was twelve, so I got pretty good at pumping floor. I used to be able to do about 120 at a time when I was in college. Obviously, as a Louie Louie Generation guy, I must admit that my push-up performance has suffered a bit since graduation day.

I used to challenge guys to one-arm push-up contests. I could always count on being able to do around thirty of them, until a few months ago when our next door neighbor Bernadette and her six-year-old daughter Emily were visiting. Emily was doing cartwheels in the living room, so I said, "Hey, Emmy, wanna see some one-arm push-ups?"

She said sure. So I got down on Mr. Floor and pushed, and nothing happened. So I pushed again. And again. Mr. Floor stayed right where he was. And Bernadette and Emily and even my Lady Wonder Wench were all standing there with their hands on their hips, rolling their eyes and looking at me like, "What are you doing down there on the floor?"

The best thing you can do in a circumstance like that is to remember what Big Louie, tells us Louie-Louie Generation guys: "If you can grin, you can win." I think he means if you suddenly find you can't do one-arm push-ups anymore—and there are ladies present—remember to laugh at yourself. By the way, laughing is a good exercise if you do it hard enough. It's like jogging inside.

There have been times when I was very glad I did all those push-ups. Last week, for example. I was called upon to be a groomsman for my buddy, Geoff. Usually that's something young guys do, but this is the second time around for Geoff, like it is for lots of Louie Louie Generation Lads and Ladies these days—so along with the wedding cake, there will be wrinkles, walkers and oxygen bottles at the reception. Geoff stands about six foot seven and weighs in at around 350. I call Geoff "Tinker Bell," which I can get away with partly because I used to do a lot of push-ups—but mostly because he knows I'm a lot faster than he is.

He is justifiably proud of his Scotch heritage, and on many formal occasions he has been known to wear a kilt featuring the family tartan. That is a sight for only the strongest among you.

Since I would be accompanying him in the wedding party, I suggested to those in authority in the proceedings that my gold lamé loincloth and purple ostrich feather would add a festive touch and it would be a good contrast to the usual drab black tuxedos. Or, at least I figured it might be a nifty occasion on which I could wear my plaid jacket that I haven't worn since high school.

For some obscure female reasons, the authorities involved, specifically my Lady W.W. and Geoff's Lady Joann disagreed. So I had to go rent a drab black tux to do whatever it is a groomsman does at a wedding.

Jasmine is the name of the attractive young lady who was working at the tux store. She carefully took my measurements—a process which I will admit I enjoyed a bit, especially the inseam part. Then she had me try on a jacket, which fit nicely on my shoulders but which had enough room in the belly part for another groomsman or, better yet, one of the bridesmaids.

I said, "What can you do about that?"

She said, "We can move some of the buttons, I guess. Our jackets are made to fit most guys your age who have pot bellies."

I cringed at the "guys your age and pot bellies" line, but then she smiled and said, "But you have the body of a twenty-five-year-old."

You cannot make this up. Well, you can, but nobody would believe you.

I grabbed Jasmine by the hand and dragged her across the store to where my Lady Wonder Wench was sitting, and I said, "Please, I beg you, tell her what you just said."

Jasmine giggled and said, "I told him we could move the buttons."

I said, "Don't trifle with me, woman, this collar around my ankle could go off at any minute."

So she giggled again, and she told my Lady Wonder Wench about my twenty-five-year-old body. I was triumphant.

Of course, my Lady Wonder Wench immediately put it into proper perspective. She said, loud enough for everyone to hear, "Right. A twenty-five-year-old's body with a four-year-old's mind."

Every woman in the store laughed and applauded.

And then they all stood up and did the wave.

27-

The Living Room's Black Hole

I'm sitting here in my big, comfortable, black-leather poppa chair, looking at a dangerous, new, thirty-two-inch-wide flat-screen hole in my living room. You can disappear down that hole—and boldly go ... nowhere. That's how lots of people join the Dreadful Dreary Drones.

As you may have figured out, I had to replace an almost perfectly good twenty-odd-year-old TV set before its time. I wanted to wait till I could afford a new 3-D TV so I could watch Catherine Zeta-Jones movies the way they were intended to be seen—through slightly steamed-up glasses. But my trusty old Zenith was driving me nuts with the closed-captioning, which it decided to turn on all by itself, and I couldn't turn it off without the original changer, which has long since joined the good old rabbit ears in Howdy Doody heaven.

I don't want to hear what most of the TV people are saying the first time around, without having to read it fifteen seconds later in a voice-recognition printout that has quietly switched the language to the Klingon setting while I wasn't watching.

I have a long history of problems with television. A long time ago, when the kids were little, I always wished there were an early morning kid's show called "Let's All Go Back to Bed and Sleep a Little Longer." It would be a puppet show like Howdy Doody. The Howdy puppet would say things like "My, it's early." Then he'd yawn and say, "I'm still tired. Let's all lie down and be very quiet till about 8:00 a.m." I think it would have been a smash hit with mommies and daddies. And daddies and mommies are where the commercial money is—but only until they hit forty-nine years old. Then they drop off the commercial cliff into what sponsors are convinced is the Dreadful Dreary Drone zone.

There was a show that understood the value of bringing Louie Louie Generation daddy viewers to kiddie shows for a while. It was called "Fun with Miss Jean." It was a half hour with Miss Jean and a bunch of kids in the studio. They played lots of games together, many of which required Miss Jean to jump up and down a lot. The fact that Miss Jean was very nicely configured, and exceptionally good at jumping up and down brought a whole new third dimension to kiddie TV and caused her show to be quite popular with daddies of all ages.

I do TV commercials for a living. Which means I'm one of those guys who have turned television into a pit of endless wants and needs. I only admit I do commercials to people I can trust. Most of the time, when people ask what I do, I just tell them, "I'm in communications." That statement, of course, communicates nothing. But I love to watch people nod as if they understand completely.

That's not to say I'm not grateful for what television commercials have done for me. For example, one of our daughters recently admitted that she was on a "sit at home and watch TV date" at her boyfriend's house a number of years ago, and things were getting a little steamy, until all of a sudden a Hartford Insurance commercial, a Sony Handy-cam commercial, and a Pep Boys commercial came on, back to back to back—with my voice on all of them—which pretty much put an end to the proceedings. So there are some good things about doing commercials.

It didn't hurt that I had taken the guy aside a few weeks before and reminded him that I was also a clinical hypnotist, and cheerfully asked how he'd feel about having a year of impotence if he put his hands on my daughter.

I may be over-possessive of my womenfolk. I don't care to share them, although I understand that's a trend now with the Pimple People. My Lady Wonder Wench used to ride her horse at a stable where there were a couple of young guys whose hormones had obviously been seriously disturbed by seeing her in jodhpurs. I jokingly mentioned to them that I was working on a new aerobatic maneuver in my little plane that was so precise that I could give a guy a vasectomy with a propeller. They all had a good laugh. But the next day, I buzzed the stable with a low fly by. That's when I had my laugh.

I like to tell you about flying my plane every once in a while. It's a little four seat prop plane, very much like most of the small planes you see at little airports. It's about as expensive as a good car. Not a fancy car, just a good car. But it does a lot of things for me. It takes me for visits with family in other states; it has shown me the top of a rainbow; and it helps me find Christmas with my Lady Wonder Wench on our traditional Christmas Eve flight. I can boldly go almost wherever I want to go in it. And that's a big help in making my life too big to tumble down that new flat-screen thirty-two-inch hole in my living room.

That screen really can be a black hole, with teeth that eat your life if you let it. It's a cleverly disguised cover for a Dreadful Dreary Drone pit. So let me pass along a suggestion from Big Louie: "Be a doer, not a viewer. Stuff your life full of real everyday miracles; a friendly smile looking back at you over a couple of cups of coffee you didn't have to make for yourself; a call you didn't expect from an old friend you haven't seen for a while; a bunch of green traffic lights on the way to work; picking the fastest line at the supermarket checkout; a sing-along with your favorite song on the radio; and finding your keys and your glasses right where you thought you left them."

Stuff stuff like that into your life, and your life will get way too big and husky to drop into that thirty-two-inch black hole. You'll never find yourself boldly going… nowhere.

28-

Glasses Guy

I've been Lawn Tractor Man, Life Guard, Pilot, Poet, Late Night Radio deejay, Hypnotist, Hunky Husband, Dad, and lots of names I won't mention. But now—as of today—I have turned into "glasses guy." Some days you're the bird, and some days you're the statue. I'm the statue today. You've probably heard about the guy who was walking down the street one day when the prescription on his glasses ran out, and he smacked right into a telephone pole. Well, today something like that happened to me.

Today was my glasses tipping point. The day I actually spent more time looking for them than I did wearing them. There's no use faking it anymore. As of today, I'm going to have to wear glasses all the time. The simple fact of the matter is that I can no longer see print any smaller than the Goodyear blimp. I can hear some of you saying, "Aw, the boobie," because you've had to wear glasses all your life. But this is new to me—and it's going to take some getting used to.

For me, this is worse than the day I found my first gray hair. You can just pluck that little sucker out and forget about it. Of course, you've got to be careful; you don't want to go nuts with that, because you could cause yourself to go prematurely bald. But from now on, if the cops ever go looking for me, they will be looking for a guy wearing small, frameless, oblong glasses. I hate that. So I said to myself, "Self, that's not me, is it? Let's do a reality check here."

So we did. And, unfortunately, the check bounced.

Some people look good in glasses. My Lady Wonder Wench is one of those people. Of course, she looks good without glasses too. When I first met her, she had pink plastic frames that had little tips at the edges, with tiny rhinestones that set off her pretty blue eyes. Steve Allen, the first Tonight Show host, had a pair of glasses with big black frames. When he wanted to emphasize a point he was making, he'd take his glasses off and point them at you.

I have a pair of Ray Ban sunglasses that I like to wear when I'm flying my little airplane. I think they make me look as if I could fly a 747 in an emergency. That's the small-plane pilot's fantasy: both pilots in the airliner's cockpit fall unconscious, and the panic-stricken flight attendant gets on the horn and asks if there is a pilot on board. And you get up, stride purposely to the cockpit, put on your Ray Bans—doesn't matter if it's midnight, appearances count—and you bring the big plane down safely on a runway. Of course, Catherine Zeta-Jones, who just happens to be aboard in first class, rushes up to you and gives you a big, sloppy kiss.

Hey, everybody is entitled to a fantasy.

I started thinking, why couldn't this work around the other way? Instead of starting to have trouble seeing, why couldn't I start becoming hard to see. Maybe I could even become invisible. Wouldn't that be fun? You could lurk anywhere and watch pretty ladies getting dressed, listen to what your friends say about you when they're driving home from your party, or check out what the car sales manager is really telling the salesman is the lowest price he's willing to take on a car you want to buy.

Then I realized that the invisibility project has already started. And it wasn't fun at all. My weight-lifter son Mark and I were walking down the beach a while ago, and a group of young lovelies in bikinis were walking along toward us. It was definitely a pull in the belly and stick out the chest moment. So I did. And they didn't even see me. I was invisible. Me … the former ocean lifeguard. All they saw was young Mr. Muscles walking along next to me.

And I started noticing that I wasn't getting noticed in supermarkets either; or restaurants; or anyplace—with one exception. There is still one way I get noticed. I was on the radio for a long time, and I've done a lot of voice-overs for television commercials, so lots of times, when I say something, people give me one of those, "Do I know you?" kind of looks, because the voice is familiar. Then they go back to ignoring me. And I hate ignorance. But, for that one moment, I still get noticed.

It used to be that when Charles Atlas showed off his muscles, he flexed his biceps. These days a six-pack of abs is the price of admission to hunk hood. How important are abs, really. I mean, except for keeping your intestines from falling in your lap, what do you do with them?

And I want you to know that I'm not questioning the importance of abs because I don't have any. I have abs. Well, actually, I have an ab. One. I found it while I was in the shower the other night. I ran right out of the shower and into the living room to show my Lady W.W. And she said, "That's wonderful, dear." But she said it in that voice that means as soon as I leave the room, she's going to call our daughter Kris and giggle with her about it.

As I recall, Superman didn't have noticeable abs. And he could fly without an airplane. He just stuck his arms out in front and said, "Up, up, and awaaaay." I always wondered if he flew in that position because he had to or if it was just something he did to impress Lois Lane. How impressed would she have been if he had flown in a sitting position—like an airline passenger reading a magazine and playing with his iPad.

And, of course, what did Superman do when he wanted to become Clark Kent, the exact opposite of Superman, a total wimp? He disguised himself as Clark Kent, the mild-mannered reporter, by putting on his glasses. He became a glasses guy. Like me.

My friends always try to put a positive spin on it. My buddy Mike is heavily into conspiracy theories and plots. He says, "Look at it this way—because you are obviously falling apart, in a hostage situation you are likely to be released first."

Thanks, Mike. What are buddies for, right?

Glasses guy. It comes with getting older. I know everybody wants to get younger. But can you imagine the horror story this world would experience if all the adults in it suddenly turned into Pimple People adolecent teenagers again?

Actually, people have started to say, "Hey, you look good, Dick." In fact, the older I get, the more people seem to be saying that. My handsomeness will probably peak the day before I die.

Glasses guy. Me. The former one-hand bra-strap-opener champ. The one time king of under the boardwalk. The late-night radio voice who would be glad to play "Misty" for the soft lady voice on the request line. I'm not aging gracefully; I know. In fact, I'm just stumbling along. But as long as I can keep those feet going, I'm not going to stop stumbling, because how else am I going to catch my Lady ? She sometimes moves pretty fast.

But it seems that the only way I can still see where I'm going now is with these damn glasses.

29-

The M. A. S. Appeal

Thanksgiving is an anniversary for me. It was on Thanksgiving night a lot of years ago that I started the "Men Are Saints" campaign on WNBC Radio. I called it the M. A. S. appeal—Men Are Saints. The idea came from remembering a special Thanksgiving while I was watching my Lady Wonder Wench and our daughter Kris, our daughter-in law Brenda, and our sister-in-law Beth scurrying around preparing dinner, while our Tall-Guy son Eric, my brother John and I were otherwise occupied, and I was struck with an actual thought.

I realized that we men are seldom given credit for our sensitivity, our intelligence, and our selfless behavior. For example, here in the Northeast, Thanksgiving is usually celebrated on a cold day. So where do we men traditionally encourage our women to spend the day? Right. In the warmest room in the house—the kitchen. While we, on the other hand, in a manly display of selfless courage, throw ourselves in front of the TV screen to protect our loved ones from the terrible effects of the cathode rays that squirt out of the picture tube. And how much credit do we men get for that traditional self-sacrifice? Right. None.

And think about this: How often have you seen a relatively innocent Louie Louie Generation guy at a raunchy bar go over to a woman he has never even met and invite her to the safety and comfort of his very own apartment to get her out of that dangerous environment? And what reward do we get? Right again. None. But we soldier on as we always have, even in the face of this shameful lack of appreciation. That's the basis for the M.A.S. appeal.

As you can imagine, the M.A.S. appeal is frequently not well received by certain people with more evolved levels of social sensitivity and mostly higher voices.

And I must confess that I am extremely thankful that the highly evolved person with a higher voice who lives with me has so far resisted giving in to the temptation that many Louie Louie ladies seem to love discussing. They sometimes refer to it as the Lorena Bobbit syndrome.

30-

Don't Do What You Don't Wanna Do Day, Do Wah, Do Wah

I was diligently drinking my morning cup of coffee today, seriously considering the possibility of starting work to finish the commercial I'd been working on for a couple of days because it's due tomorrow morning, when the phone rang. I put the half-full coffee cup down next to the computer, kicked my chair back, tripped on the rug, and as I grabbed the desk to keep from falling down, I knocked the coffee into the computer keyboard.

The call was from a telemarketer. And it was recorded. I hit the callback button on the phone to ream the company out, and a phone company recording said the number was out of service. I walked over to the kitchen to grab a paper towel to sop up the coffee, forgetting that I had used the last of the roll last night. Fortunately, I was wearing an old shirt, so I looked around to be sure my Lady Wonder Wench had really gone to the supermarket, and I reverted to my bachelor days. I pulled the shirt up out of my trousers and started wiping up the coffee. But in the process of trying to get the coffee out from between the computer keys, I must have hit the delete button. The commercial I was going to finish writing disappeared from the screen, replaced by a notice that said I was trying to perform an illegal operation, and therefore the program would close down to protect the computer, and I should see the network administrator.

So, I'm standing there with my shirt soaked with coffee, steam pouring out of my ears, and saying some very naughty words, and the front door opens and my next door neighbor's little kid walks in to sell me some Girl Scout cookies. That's when the business phone rings, and it's a guy from a network of daytime only radio stations wanting to sell me some commercial time on their most popular show, which is about canning vegetables.

It was definitely time to take a deep breath and sit down, here in my big, comfortable, black-leather poppa chair in my living room. So I did. And I'm still here. And I think I'd better stay here for a while and calm down. I'm getting to like sitting here, calming down. It gives me something to do. I'm getting to like it so much that I'm going to make a point of doing it at least once a month. Maybe more often than that. I'm going to call it my "Don't Do What You Don't Wanna Do Day, do wah, do wah."

I was going to call it my "Do Exactly What You Wanna Do Day," but sometimes things I can't control happen, which makes doing exactly what I want to do impossible on that particular day. For example, sometimes I want to take the day off and go flying in my little airplane, but there's a thunderstorm. Or sometimes I want to watch the New York Mets play baseball, but it's January. And worst of all, occasionally my Lady comes down with a headache. So it's "Don't Do What You Don't Wanna Do Day, do wah, do wah." And it's "wanna" not "want to" because some days I don't want to prissy around with proper diction.

We need some research in order to make future future "Don't Do What You Don't Wanna Do Days, do wah, do wah" work out. And Big Louie has come up with some good ideas. For example, a great way to start your day would be by just going back to bed. Or you could slip some popping corn into your pancake mix. That way maybe the pancakes will flip over by themselves and you won't have to do it. If you're going through a revolving door, do it on the push from the guy in front of you.

You may feel the urge to do some research of your own on the subject. If you do, and you want to send me the results, my e-mail address is dick@dicksummer.com. If you don't want to send me the results, just sit there and tell me, "It's one of my Don't Do What You Don't Wanna Do Days, so do wah, do wah to you, Dick Summer."

I have been sitting here so long, a little while longer and I could be declared a registered landmark. I guess I could cop out and say I'm meditating. But I kind of like the idea of telling people, "Hey, this is my Don't Do What You Don't Wanna Do Day, do wah, do wah."

And if anybody says I'm just wasting time, I'll tell them what Big Louie always says. "It is better to have loafed and lost, than never to have loafed at all."

31-

Richard's Riot

As any honest Louie Louie Generation guy will admit, one of the good things about having some years in your rearview mirror is that eventually you learn when to say yes, when to say no, when to say EEE-HAA, and when to say whoops. My Lady Wonder Wench saw a very loud EEE-HAA moment coming this morning, and she cut it short with just one word: "Richard." When she says Richard like that, it always gets my attention. My Lady Wonder Wench is the only person in the world, besides the IRS, the FAA, and the Department of Motor Vehicles, who calls me Richard. And that's only when my testosterone has betrayed me, and I do something that can best be described as adolescent, immature, and or smarmy. I have to admit that I hit the trifecta jackpot this morning.

Here's what happened: I'm having some dental work done that involves a dentist and three nurses, so it's not just the everyday kind of dental work where he says things like "Open wide, this won't hurt," "Can you feel it when I whack you with my dental hammer," and "Please don't bite down; that's my thumb." It's more complicated than that. So my Lady Wonder Wench decided that it would be a good idea for her to drive me home, because there would be so much Novocain in my mouth that I wouldn't be able to see over my swollen upper lip to drive home myself. That's why she was sitting in the office with me when the thirteen-year-old Pimple Person Princess nurse came in to take my blood pressure and to ask questions that are routine in a procedure like this—questions like "Are you allergic to penicillin," and "What's the name of anyone you'd like to have us call in case you die?"

When she asked who she should call in case I die, one of those voices you probably also have in your head that insists on telling you jokes at a funeral made me say, "In an emergency, please call Sophia Loren." Nurse Pimple Person Princess didn't even blink; she just wrote it down because she had no idea that Sophia Loren lurks and smiles and turns up the sweat glands in the dreams and fantasies of almost every Louie Louie Generation guy.

And then Nurse Pimple Person Princess said the most amazing thing anybody has ever said to me in a dentist's office—or, actually, anywhere. You will not believe this.

With a completely straight face, Nurse P.P.P. said, quote, "I'll tell the girls you're ready now."

I'll tell the girls you're ready now!

Instantly, a soundtrack featuring lots of slow drum rolls started in my mind. And on cue, a long line of Victoria's Secret models appeared, led by ladies with names like Fifi and Desiree and a mostly naked Catherine Zeta-Jones look-alike who had, for who knows how long, been lying in wait, anxiously anticipating the word that I was ready for them. They whirled into the room and began to have their way with me. The voice in my head started hollering and clapping his hands like a Spanish tango dancer. Or maybe I was really clapping my hands over my head—things were getting confused—when all of a sudden a very familiar voice rang out with a very specific message. It said, "Richard."

Whoops.

As Big Louie, his own bad self, the chief mustard cutter of the Louie Louie Generation, has explained in the past, testosterone is a preservative. A preservative is a chemical that keeps fungus and other things from growing. Growing is another word for maturing. And evidently, I seem to have an excess of that testosterone stuff.

All this happened very quickly. And no sooner had the sound of the word "Richard" made my eyes flick open, when what to my wondering eyes should appear, but "the girls" Nurse Pimple Person Princess had promised. They weren't exactly the same ones who had starred in that silken, sweaty, sleazy scene that had evidently put the smile on my face—the smile that my Lady later probably accurately described as smarmy. There were three of them, masked and wearing surgical gowns that were not slit up the side. There was not a stitch of black lace showing, which in their case was probably just as well. Two of them were Pimple People. As a matter of fact, one still had acne, and one had distinctly noticeable droopy ears and things, and the non–pimple person would have looked much more natural wearing orthopedic boots and corrective hot pants.

Then the dentist walked in, stuck a yard long needle full of Novocain in my gums, and said, "This won't hurt." I wanted to tell him it already did.

But then the Novocain hit, and I couldn't make my upper lip move.

Do you know you can't say whoops, whoopee, wait a minute, or any other word that begins with a w when you have a lip full of Novocain?

Twy it.

32-

Wage Baseball, Not War

I grew up in Brooklyn, which has been a National League baseball town ever since there was a ballpark called Ebbets Field on a Brooklyn street called Bedford Avenue. I'm a Mets fan now—for my sins. So when my Lady Wonder Wench came to live with me in New York, we spent a lot of time at Shea Stadium. You know I call her my Lady Wonder Wench. But this is the story of one beautiful early Summer day when she also became my "Baseball Babe."

Since we moved to Pennsylvania, we've been watching the Mets play in the Phillies beautiful new stadium, where the parking costs something just short of the national debt, hot dogs go for about seven dollars a bite, and the only way you can get a ticket is if someone leaves it to you in his will. The Philly fans remind me a lot of the good old Ebbets Field crowds. Local legend has it that a fan fell out of the upper deck last year, and when he was able to get up and walk away, the crowd booed. Just like home.

We were at a game last year, and a couple of guys were sitting next to us and really screaming. I said to one of them, "Hey, guys, cool it. My wife is here, and you're making me uncomfortable."

He turned to me, noticed my Mets cap, spilled some beer on my shoe, and said, "This is war."

I said, "No, this is a game. When a war is over, you count how many guys got killed. When this game is over, these guys will take a shower and ride their limos to some five-star restaurant and have dinner together."

The guy spilled some beer on my other shoe and went back to screaming. I rolled my scorecard up and was about to stick it in his nearest private place, but my Lady Wonder Wench gave me one of those, "Do that, and I'm leaving" looks, so I didn't. Probably just as well. Some times I think I'm tougher than I really am. Baseball Babe. She's always watching my back.

I really hate it when people get nuts like that about sports.

But I love competition. Baseball is a game of skill, of course, so I wasn't really very good at it. But I was a very successful high school swimmer, because I swam the butterfly. And the way you win a butterfly swimming race is by simply refusing to quit on the third lap, which is the place in the race where you'd rather die than pull your arms out of their sockets and over your head one more time.

When I was at WNBC Radio, we had a softball team we called the Cheaters. We called it that because we cheated. We told people up front—honestly—that we were going to cheat, so it was okay. I am convinced that the only game you can't cheat at is peek-a-boo. The WNBC Cheaters played charity games against cops and fire departments—once against the Playboy Bunnies, and once against some nuns, believe it or not. Mostly, we lost, but I always claimed we won 9–2 on the air, because, as I said, we cheated. The nuns cheated, too—they prayed. And they took advantage of a very important thing that I'll try to put delicately: Where do you apply the tag on a nun who is about to slide into second while she's saying the Lord's Prayer and brandishing a rosary with a twenty-pound crucifix on it?

Of course, no matter how skillful and athletic some women might become, no woman will ever play major league baseball, for several important reasons. First and foremost, women do not spit, nor do they scratch. And that's a good part of the game at the major-league level. Also, as you've probably heard, if a woman was playing third base and had to choose between catching a pop foul fly ball or saving the life of a kid falling from the stands, she would catch the kid without even considering the fact that she might have started a double play with a good peg to second.

I don't play much ball anymore. Like lots of Louie Louie Generation guys, I have developed kind of a furniture problem. My chest has fallen into my drawers. Our bodies are like bars of soap. They get worn down when they get sent to the showers so often. That's why Louie Louie Generation guys have to turn the charm up to stun to remain the partners of choice of super models and Baseball Babes everywhere.

It's a tough job, but somebody has to do it. Attitude/gratitude. Happy, healthy and hot.

33-

The Emerald City

Vegas is a shining example of the fact that guys cannot look at a half-naked woman and think at the same time. That doesn't mean we're stupid. It just means that because of that pesky testosterone, we tend to act stupid—even highly sophisticated guys such as Bill Clinton and myself.

By the way, let me make an important point here. I usually talk about Louie Louie guys and girls—I seldom use the terms men and women. People have complained about that. Lemme 'splain: I seldom think of myself as a man. I'm a guy, and the song Louie Louie has been an important part of the sound track of my life. Therefore, I am proud to be a Louie Louie Generation guy. And I don't call my Lady Wonder Wench a woman. She's my girlfriend. People who always insist on being called men or women need to relax. As Big Louie always says, "You people have gotta grab a grin." You need more double 'tude. Happy, healthy and hot.

I can't understand why so many people are hurtling down the path to holier-than-thou-ness. It's as if grown-up, dignified, stuffy men and women have this haunting fear that somewhere, someone may actually be laughing.

Look at it this way: it was a group of grown-up and totally dignified men who got us to the moon. What did they do when they got there? They hit golf balls. Ten zillion dollars for one round of golf. On the other hand, it was probably some guy who just got fired who invented mooning. Let me ask you, which is the cheaper and far more practical activity in our everyday lives?

I do like the word I saw on the men's room door at the Dallas airport though: "Hombre". That sounds like a guy with a serious Western wardrobe who knows how to mosey his way around the square-dance floor with the ladies. Hombre is a good word for a Louie Louie Generation guy.

But the word woman always reminds me of my Aunt Eva, who was a good woman in the absolutely worst sense of the word. She would always pick, pick, pick: "Don't let the dog lick your face." "Put that BB gun away; you'll put somebody's eye out." "Don't spit in your soup." (I wasn't spitting in my soup. I was just blowing on it to cool it off. But I seriously considered spitting in her soup.)

And to further confound the Politically Correct Forces for Good in the Community, I have always really liked the word girl. Expensive, professional people who know things—psychologists and talk show hosts, for example—would probably tell you that it's an association that I must have made back in kindergarten when, at one wonderful recess, I discovered that people like Jeannie Campbell weren't just soft boys. They were called "girls."

Just this past week, in Vegas, I was sitting by the pool and a James Bond-type girl wriggled past with high heels, sunglasses, and her little poodle. She had on a tiny black thong bikini under a transparent black-lace blouse, her long blonde hair was swept up and held in place by a fancy comb. It was just like "The Girl from Ipanema," every guy she passed said Ahhhhhh. (By the way, if they had called that song the "Woman from Ipanema," it wouldn't have been a hit. Hell, it wouldn't have even fit the rhythm of the rhyme.)

My Lady Wonder Wench was right there, and she didn't mind that gurgling sound I must have been making, in fact, she giggled, and that is such a lovely sound. And she knows I wouldn't swap her giggle for any other girl's wriggle.

The Vegas girl who made the biggest impression on me was Bettina, the Hover Dam tour-bus driver. She's about five feet tall and probably weighs in at around ninety-nine pounds, and she could sling that big bus around like it was a tricycle. She was a funny, professional, single mom with five kids. I remember she was pointing out a big house belonging to Celine Dion, and Bettina was saying Ms. Dion is starring in one of the shows in town, and I was thinking; "Girl, if you want to see a real star, tilt your rearview mirror down and take a look at yourself." At the end of the tour, two people stiffed her—didn't give her a tip—but she smiled at them anyway. Lady Wonder Wench and I double tipped her.

We saw the Celine Dion show. It was weird. Ms. Dion is a modestly talented singer with a somewhat screechy voice, a bit of a French accent that has obviously made her a huge star with people from Montreal, and a high-powered merchandising campaign. Right inside the entrance to the theater was a life-size statue of Ms. Dion, and for a significant financial consideration, a photographer would take your picture with the statue, and you could tell the folks back home that you and Celine were just hanging out one evening. What happens in Vegas, isn't necessarily what people think happens in Vegas.

But the highlight of the trip for me was a little two-year-old kid by the name of Trey. Trey's dad and mom are friends of ours who live in LA. They came out to visit while we were in town. Trey's real name is Robert—Robert Anthony—but he is the third-generation Robert in the family, so everybody calls him Trey. He looks exactly like his dad, right down to the expressions on his face and the way he walks—kind of a strut that leans from one side to the other, every time he takes a step.

Being two, Trey understands that the entire world was made just so he'd have someplace to explore, and like any healthy two-year-old boy, he sometimes explores pretty fast in some very unpredictable directions. One of the cocktail waitresses caught his eye. As I said, he's a lot like his dad. Anyway, he peeled off in one of those high-speed two-year-old scoots right into the casino, and I caught him, hoisted him up on my shoulder, and he did that two-year-old laugh. A big, loud, combination squeal, wiggle, and giggle.

It was just an instant that Trey won't remember. But I will. It was the highlight of my trip. I liked being a dad, all those Louie Louie years ago.

34-

Here's Looking at You, Kid

Once upon a time, a pretty, talented young lady by the name of Connie Francis sang a tune called "Stupid Cupid." If you're a member of the Louie Louie Generation, you probably remember it well. In honor of Valentine's Day, I took a very unscientific poll of a bunch of friends of mine, and the results shocked me. More than 90 percent of them—both sexes—just blew off Valentine's Day. One guy even said, "That cupid stuff is just stupid."

No. It's not.

I like Valentine's Day. I've had enough of Cupid's arrows stuck in my backside to resupply the Indians at Custer's Last Stand. And some of those arrows really hurt. But as Big Louie always says, "Kiss the boo-boo, learn a lesson, and move on. Or better yet, get someone to kiss the boo-boo for you."

The first arrow Cupid shot at me had the name Jeanie Campbell written on it. She was six, and I was seven. It hurt a little, and I didn't even understand why. But it taught me that I could take a little hurting, even the kind I didn't understand. It sure wasn't stupid. It was an important lesson. Through the years some of that little guy's arrows, with other names on them, went pretty deep.

Lots of boo-boos needed to be kissed. Fortunately, my Lady Wonder Wench is the number one boo-boo kisser in the world. Well, my world anyway.

One of the guys I talked to said, "I'm too old for that kind of thing."

Big Louie went nose to nose with that guy. You know what Louie says about when you still have some moving parts left: "move 'em."

I like Valentine's Day. Sometimes you get to tell somebody, "I love you." And maybe you'll get to hear it back. Lots of times, it gets sexy. It comes at the beginning of baseball's spring training season. "My Funny Valentine" is a great tune. What's not to like?

There's a history to Valentine's Day. It seems there was a priest by the name of Valentinus, who lost his head courtesy of Claudius the Cruel on February 14th in the year 269 AD. Supposedly, Father V. healed his jailer's blind daughter, fell in love with her, and left a note for her in his cell the night before his execution. The note said, "I love you. From your Valentine."

Most holy people get a little uncomfortable about romance. Especially the kind where there are fingers and flesh involved. One Christian website has come up with an idea to keep our minds off our fingers and flesh by selling "Valentine's Day cards from God." It seems to me that we simple Louie Louie Generation guys would call God excessively stiff competition. No pun intended.

And the Pickle Puss People have come up with a competing day for folks who don't want any part of romance. They call it "Singles Awareness Day." The initials of Singles Awareness Day, I think appropriately, are SAD. I think SAD is … sad. Men and women belong together. There are some exceptions of course, and God bless them too. Let's just say lovers belong together.

"Relationship" is sometimes a badly used word. Businesses have relationships. Lovers have romances. A relationship develops. A romance explodes. A relationship makes progress. A romance makes sweat. Mutual sweating helps the people who are doing the mutual sweating to stick with each other.

Once upon a time, there was a pre–Louie Louie Generation guy who was injured in a fist fight in the Navy. The guy had a funny name. The injury left him with a slight lisp. He had big ears too. Not exactly the makings of a career as a movie star. But that's what he became. The biggest movie star of his time. His name was Humphrey Bogart.

Some younger Louie Louie Generation folks may not remember him. But the rest of us will never forget him, especially on Valentine's Day. He made a lot of movies. But mostly we remember an old black-and-white film called Casablanca. One of the things that made the film successful was that it featured a tune that I hope will never go away. "You must remember this, a kiss is still a kiss, a sigh is just a sigh. The fundamental things apply, as time goes by." Bogart and his costar Ingrid Bergman really got it right in Casablanca.

In one scene, he looked at Bergman, who was possibly the most beautiful woman in the world at the time. He looked right at her, for a long time, then he smiled that crooked smile and he said, "Here's looking at you, kid." And they cut to a tight shot of Bergman's face as she filled the screen with her eyes.

Cupid isn't stupid. And as every Louie-Louie Generation lad and lady has experienced a few times, the little guy's arrows can be weapons of mass destruction. But I think if you like the idea of doing some serious mutual sweating—and sticking together—you may have to take a chance and change your tune. If "Stupid Cupid" isn't going to do it for you, try that tune The Association did; they called it "Cherish." You don't hear that word very much anymore. It's a good word. And slightly sweaty.

Or, if you're a really big fan of the mutual sweats, turn up the steam and get into that tune The Troggs did: "Wild Thing (You Make My Heart Sing)." Or better yet, Peggy Lee's "Fever."

Unfortunately, according to my "Stupid Cupid" poll, an awful lot of people, even some in good relationships, have, in the words of The Righteous Brothers, "lost that lovin' feeling." It's a big loss. A terrible quiet. An awful power failure.

Do you suppose some of this Valentine's Day put down trend is due to a lack of guts? Are so many people just afraid to stand up and tell Cupid to take his best shot?

I know that sometimes when you're the only one of the "Wild Things" left in the wreckage of a romance it hurts. Bad. But even if you've lost that lovin' feeling, you haven't lost everything.

Remember that gorgeous song from the musical Cats: "Memories, all alone in the moonlight, I can smile at the old days; I was beautiful then. I remember the time I knew what happiness was. Let the memories live again."

Memories count too.

So thanks, Jeannie Campbell.

Wherever you are.

35-

Beam Me Outta Here, Scotty

The job has been driving me nuts. So have the kids and grandkids. Nothing but bad news on TV. And my feet hurt. It's been that kind of week. I was thinking I need a change of scene—fast. It was definitely time to tell Scotty to beam me up. Come on, Scotty, zap me. Get me out of here. That's what I was thinking, and all of a sudden, Zap! I saw a quick window of opportunity. And I opened it, and I stuck my left elbow out through it.

Here's what happened: I was grousing around my office, working on a new commercial that wasn't working. That's the way it sometimes goes with my day job. It was a gorgeous, sunshiny, spring day in the neighborhood, and I got this terrible urge to play hooky from work right in the middle of the day. And I did it. I got in the car and started off for the airport. I haven't been flying my little airplane very much lately. I miss that, and as I said, it was a day full of spring sunshine and blue skies. So I hit the highway. And without thinking, I did something I haven't done in years.

Only Louie-Louie Generation folks will understand this. I was zooming down the highway and I popped all four windows, slid the sun roof back, turned up the bluesy Tom Jones CD to stun, and I stuck my left elbow out the window … and it must have been exactly the window of opportunity that I was looking for, because all of a sudden, my whole world went Zap!

The Pimple People would never understand. They've always had air conditioning in their cars. They have no idea what it's like to stick your left elbow out the window and feel the wind slide up your sleeve and mess up your hair while you let the sunlight and the music and the laughs tear away a lot of years. They haven't been around for a lot of years. And the idea would never occur to the Dreadful Dreary Drones. They might get their hair all messed up. But for a few magical minutes, this Louie-Louie guy wasn't worried about his job, or the kids, or the bad news on TV, or even my aching feet. When I stuck my elbow out that window, for a few magic minutes I was a happy, eighteen-year-old, sun-tanned, Coney Island lifeguard hunk again—for just a little while. The double 'tude was pumping. I was happy, healthy, and hot.

I got to the airport, pulled my little airplane out of the hanger, strapped her on, fired her up, bounced down the runway, and zoomed up into a lot of blue sky and bright sunshine. I took just a few turns around the airport, wiggled my wings at a couple of pretty girls riding horses, and came in for one of those landings when you're not quite sure when the wheels actually touch down. Perfect.

Good window-of-opportunity zaps like that usually happen in threes, and this one did too. Bill, our mail guy, arrived a few minutes after I got home. Along with the usual catalogs and bills, he had a business envelope and a box from an address I didn't recognize. The box was from proud podcast participant "California Dennis," the transplanted New Yorker. It seems I was talking about good kid things in the podcast last week, and Dennis sent me a yo-yo. Zap! Another window opened. I stuck my elbow through that window too. Actually I stuck my finger through it. I tied the string around my third finger (that's called your signal finger in Brooklyn), and I flipped my wrist and the yo-yo went down, took a quick "sleep," and came up again, just like it used to. Thank you, Dennis.

I got so excited that I made the mistake of rushing upstairs to show my Lady Wonder Wench. I flipped my wrist again and pulled the string, just like I used to, but this time I only got a "yo" out of the "yo-yo." It just went to sleep and stayed there instead of climbing up again—while she was watching. Performance anxiety got to me, I guess. But she didn't slam the happy window closed. She just rolled her eyes, put her hands on her hips, and gave me that "He'll never grow up, but I love him anyway" Louie Louie Lady smile. You know, like wives do—if you're lucky enough to have one like my Lady W.W..

The third window-of-opportunity zap was in the envelope. My lower reptilian limbic system brain went on maximum red overdrive when I opened it. It was our tickets to each of the last few New York Mets spring training games in Port St. Lucie. I love the Mets. I love baseball. And I love Port St. Lucie. It's God's waiting room. I'm the youngest guy in town every year when we go there for spring training. Port St. Lucie looks like Halloween every day. If you can cross the street without oxygen, during only one red light, everybody starts cheering. You can hear them: "All the way, yea, yea, yea. All the way, yea, yea, yea." Then they bang their canes and walkers on the pavement for you and offer you a drag on their personal oxygen generators.

Thanks, Scotty. Zap! Zap! Zap!

36-

Lazy, Crazy, Hazy Days

L ife is like a giant roll of toilet paper. The closer it gets to the end, the faster it goes. That's one of the truest statements ever made by Big Louie, his own bad self. It's hard to believe, but it's time for the end of this year's "Lazy, Crazy, Hazy Days" of "Saturdays In the Park," "Talkin' Baseball," with the "Summer Wind" blowing in the hair of the girls in "Itsy, Bitsy, Teenie, Weenie, Yellow Polkadot Bikinis," as they're "Walking in the Sand" on sweaty Summer Days and lounging around watching the fireworks with you from "Under the Boardwalk" on Soft Summer Nights.

Where I grew up in Brooklyn, when there were no more pencils, no more books, no more teacher's dirty looks, it was stickball, kick the can, The Cyclone Roller Coaster and the Parachute Jump at Coney Island, Italian ice cups, hanging on the stoop with some of the guys singing doo-wop, cheap dates on the Staten Island ferry that was a short cruise from Brooklyn to Staten Island for about a quarter. The Mets and the Yanks and Fourth of July fireworks that stretched for miles along the harbor and parades with Seventy Six Trombones and the absolutely most beautiful girls in the world wearing their summer dresses.

A long time ago, when I was a lifeguard on Bay 22 at Coney Island, I had a quick lesson about women one Summer day. I had a girlfriend by the name of Matilda. Red hair, blue eyes, smart, and sweet. She used to make me lunch, and bring it down to the beach with her. One day, I went out to bring in a swimmer who was having trouble, and I used a life guard technique called the cross chest carry. In this case, the swimmer happened to be a rather attractive young lady, and in the process of bringing her in, the top of her bathing suit slipped rather drastically. I swear in this particular instance I had no control over the situation. The surf was pretty big at the time, and I had all I could do to swim in against a pretty tough undertow. But as I'm sure Big Louie could have predicted, just as I helped the girl out of the water and she was hastily adjusting her bathing suit who shows up? Matilda of course. She took one look, ripped the sandwiches she had made out of their wrappers, and threw them on the sand, stepped on them and stormed out of my life.

I've told my Lady Wonder Wench about this in the interests of full disclosure, and because if I didn't a couple of my wise guy buddies probably would have mentioned it anyway, and she actually took Matilda's side. Honest to God I was innocent. That time. Every time I claim innocence about anything I get the strangest look from Ms. Wench.

If you're a member of the Louie-Louie Generation, you remember before cars had air conditioning, and people drove around with their elbows stuck out the windows trying to get some air and looking cool. When I was a disk jockey in those days, it was kind of neat to pull up to the guy next to you at a stop light, and listen to hear if he had your station on his radio. Or walking down the beach hearing your station on the portable radios playing The Jamies "Summertime, Summertime," or the Spoonful's "Summer in the City", or the Drifters' "Up on the Roof."

Some people didn't understand "Up on the Roof." In New York and some other big cities, the rooftops were called "tar beach." And folks who couldn't get away for the day, but could grab an hour, would go up there to get a tan. Lots of times the dress code was optional, which is why I think a lot of guys learned to fly helicopters.

Back in Indianapolis. I did a show on WIBC radio from a studio that was built for me on top of a drive in restaurant called "Merril's Hi-Decker." In the Summertime, we had local bands come in, and we'd broadcast them live from the parking lot almost every night. And we played Make it or Break It with new records, and teased the Car Hops about their sexy Summer-short-shorts. In Boston at WBZ, every Summer, we'd broadcast almost all day from a trailer we called the Sundeck Studio at Nantasket beach. We had ice cube tossing contests, and hot dog eating contests, and wet bikini scavenger hunts for goofy prizes like crazy feet. They were big plastic things that looked a little like swim fins, but they had big ugly toes painted on the tops.

We were all some kind of "Sunshine Supermen" back then. The Summers were long, and the loving was Summer sweaty and good.

Louie Louie Generation folks are now in the early Autumn of our lives. It's a good time to be alive. We're still mostly happy, healthy and hot. But there are flecks of gold on the leaves, and squadrons of birds are headed south, and the days are getting a little short.

So let's catch every bit of Summer-Lovin' that's left.

37-

Soft Summer Sounds

I'm listening to the soft sounds of the Summer night creatures. In fact, I just recorded them. They're so ... calm. I need to calm down sometimes. Everybody does. I think I'll have some fun with the recording too. We'll be having some folks over for New Year's Eve again this year, and I think I'll put the summer night creatures sound on the stereo while they're bouncing the ball in Times Square. I like watching my friends' brains spin a little. It must tickle, because it makes them giggle. And giggles are good for calming down.

The smart guys in the white lab coats say that these Summer night creature sounds are made by the little male bug dudes rubbing their back legs together to attract their little foxy lady bugs—much like you see at your neighborhood singles bar on a Friday night. But listen to that sound. Are you telling me that all that sound is made by some little one-ounce bug? He'd have to be one heck of a bug stud. Seems to me that to make all that noise, you'd need at least a hundred-pound cricket, and excuse me, Jimminy Cricket fans, but a hundred-pound cricket is just an ugly thought.

My Lady Wonder Wench says that if you kill a cricket in the house, a woman will get pregnant. I killed one in the house last night. I am watching carefully to see what kind of effect that has on my Lady Wonder Wench. I have suggested to her that if she wants to get pregnant, and killing the cricket doesn't work, I know of some alternate methods.

I am not a big bug fan. In the sixties, chocolate-covered ants were all the rage for a while. Ants disguised as chocolate bars do not tempt my palate at all. Our kids liked to collect fireflies in jars. They were brought up in the suburbs. I'm from Brooklyn. There are no fireflies in Brooklyn any more. That's either because they have been overcollected through the years by lots and lots of Brooklyn kids or because very little besides cement grows in Brooklyn.

When our kids started collecting fireflies in jars, they always thought the fireflies looked so pretty in there—and they did. I always resisted the temptation to tell the kids that all living creatures have to breathe, and stuffing a firefly into a jar was going to have serious side effects on his ability to light up our lives in the very near future. I say his ability because I think the flies that light up are males, trying to attract females. Again, just like in the singles bars.

Why is it always the guys who have to attract the girls—except for certain odd-exception guys, and we'll just call them the Clooney crowd. Why is it that if a guy walks into a singles bar, rubs his back legs together, and asks ten women for their phone numbers, he's going to strike out at least nine out of ten times? If a woman walks into a singles bar and rubs her back legs together, she wouldn't have time to ask for a phone number before nine out of ten guys were trying to light up her life.

I like spinning people brains a little because it must tickle. Tickles make giggles. And I like giggles. Giggles are good. Yesterday, I opened a window, looked up at the sky, and smiled. My Lady Wonder Wench said, "Why did you do that?"

I told her it was "because that satellite might be up there snapping pictures." That's what she gets for paying attention when

I was rubbing my back legs together at the radio station in Boston where we both worked, all those years ago.

I like making her giggle—my Lady Wonder Wench Summer. In fact, her giggle is my favorite Summer sound.

38-

A Double 'Tude for Christmas

"Silent Night" is the world's number one Christmas song. But "Jingle Bells" is the song you hear most often on the all-Christmas music stations. Most of the commercials use it for production music—that's the music that plays under the commercials. Which is interesting, because "Jingle Bells" is not really about Christmas. It's about people having fun together during a sleigh ride.

Lots of people say Christmas isn't about Christ's birthday anymore. They've got a point. The shopping has gone nuts. We've got kids looking for a reindeer with a red nose in the night instead of the Star of Bethlehem. And worst of all, deeply religious people are killing each other over who best knows God's way to bring peace to the world. Definitely not what a loving Creator would have had in mind. So what is Christmas if it's not about Christ's birthday? I have some ideas about that:

The Salvation Army volunteers are out again this year, some of them bravely blowing trumpets right into the winter wind, and others just ringing a little bell and smiling. They don't do it for pay. They do it for Christmas. For some people passing by, that Salvation

Army volunteer's smile is the only smile they'll see on a real person that day.

One winter a long time ago, the Salvation Army rescued Christmas for a little girl in Boston by seeing to it that she had a doll and a good turkey dinner. That little girl grew up to become my Lady Wonder Wench. Thank you for that, Christmas, whatever you are.

My dad was a church choir master in Brooklyn. He had forty men and more than fifty women in his choir. He always had people of different backgrounds sing a carol from their "old country." Tanya was a short, smiley, Louie Louie Generation lady who sang, "The Carol of the Bells," because her family came here from Russia. Jack was a skinny guy who had a graphics business. His family was from England, so he sang, "What Child is This?"

My grandfather came to Midnight Mass one year. He left his home in Germany just before World War II because he saw Hitler coming and he wasn't having any part of what that meant. That was the year I sang "Stille Nacht" with Dad's choir. It brought Grosspapa home for a moment. His tears were bittersweet. That's the way it is sometimes when you go home … only for a moment. But it's always good to go home—even if it's just for a moment. He was a good, loving, hard, proud man. I remember that his Christmas tree had real candles one long ago Christmas. Thank you for that memory, Christmas.

Dad took his whole choir caroling all around the neighborhood every year on the week before Christmas. Whole blocks full of people would gather around the choir and sing along; Christians, Jews, Muslims, Buddhists, Pagans, and Atheists. They all sang. And smiled. And wished each other well. That memory rates another thank-you, Christmas.

The pope and his priests, including my cousin Father Damian, will pray for peace. As will the preachers, and the rabbis and good people everywhere. A couple of people by the name of Donna Sheehan and Paul Reffel are taking a different approach. They're trying to get everybody in the world to make love for peace on December 22, the first night of winter. Lots of people are laughing at Donna and Paul, and some people are shocked—shocked, I tell you, and possibly even incensed, and I wouldn't be surprised if a few people tried to have them arrested for promoting immorality. Donna and Paul will be called a couple of publicity-seeking nuts. But I think they're on to something much more important than that.

Christmas is big enough and magical enough to include Christ's birthday party, a little girl's doll, turkey dinner, Santa Claus, and a reindeer with a red nose, wide-screen TVs, and "Jingle Bells," so maybe it's big enough and magical enough to even include pagans. Magic is a pagan tradition. That's where we got the Christmas tree and the Yule log. If you're a pagan, you'll recognize Donna and Paul's idea of making love on the first night of winter as part of a ritual that was sacred long before any religion we'll celebrate this Christmas even existed. One of our daughters and a close friend are pagans. So I hope—and pray—that Christmas really isn't just about Christ's birthday anymore.

My Lady Wonder Wench and I went for our traditional Christmas flight in our little airplane the other night. We have a little four-seat airplane that flies low and slow. Most of our friends think we go out looking for Santa Claus every year. But that's not what we're doing. I guess you could say we're looking for some kind of magic Christmas gold. And we found it again this year.

Our little airport is a few miles west of Philly. As usual on a cold, clear, pretty-close-to-Christmas night, when my Lady and I got there it was dark and deserted except for the white runway lights, the blue taxi way lights, the spotlight on the wind sock, and the revolving beacon on top of the hanger. We strapped ourselves in, fired up the engine, and climbed up into the black-and-white magic midnight.

If you heard a small plane engine late the other night and looked up and saw small wingtip lights playing in the stars that might have been us. Moonlight was shining into the cockpit; the city's Christmas lights were sliding under our wings.

Those city lights were Santa Claus bright. You could almost hear the hustling and the ho-ho-ho-ing from all the crowds, and the music and the parties going on down there. But that's not what we were looking for. We were looking for…magic. Christmas gold.

So we turned out over the suburbs…the lights get gentler out there. Instead of the city hustle and bustle, and the Santa Claus jingle-bell sounds, you get houses carefully decorated with Christmas lights, and there's a feeling of carols playing softly on stereos, and fancy paper wrapping around personal presents, and cups of hot chocolate with cold whipped cream, and kids trying to pretend they're really asleep.

Then, a little farther out we floated over some farms, mostly Amish with no electricity…so they had real candles in the windows. There were a few horse-drawn wagons on the dark roads, their lanterns slowly swinging from side to side. It was like flying backward in time. It was quiet. So quiet.

My Lady was sitting in the right seat, looking like a lovely little girl, wearing those big copilot headphones in the moonlit cockpit. She started to smile…and then she started to cry. And that's when she did it. Again. She said, "Thank you for this. I love you."

And right there, in our little plane's cockpit, the black-and-white midnight turned to Christmas gold.

The Christmas magic. We found it again.

Thank you Christmas.

Thank you, whatever you are.

39-

Stealth Stuff

Stealth stuff is slowly stalking me—sneaking up on me—smothering everything in its path. Stealth stuff sneaks in under your radar. That's why it's called stealth stuff.

Stealth stuff sprouts on smooth flat surfaces like tables, the tops of dressers, and kitchen counters. Yesterday, when I got back from the store with my nifty, new, all-frequency desk lamp, which will give me healthy virtual sunlight during the darker months; my new Wi-Fi transmitter, which will let me use my laptop anywhere within a five-mile radius; and my new ten-terabyte external hard drive, made in China and assembled in Thailand, my stealth-stuff signal finally went off. It was alerting me to the startling scope of the danger I face from the rapidly accelerating level of stealth stuff that has evidently for years been stalking me, sneaking up on me. But it may be too late.

I work at my day job in my home office. But that deadly stealth stuff has now completely covered my desk, so where am I going to put the brand-new stuff I just bought? I found myself standing there yesterday, looking at where I last remembered seeing my desk, with the stuff I just bought still in my hands, when I heard the phone. It took me ten rings to find it, covered—no, buried—under huge heaps of sinister, stealthy stuff.

I started thinking that I should be thankful that I could still find my own personal self. So I figured at least with my personal body, I was still one step ahead of the stealth stuff. But that's when I realized I was standing there with more new stuff, sneakily stuffing itself into both of my hands.

A certain Louie-Louie lady who lives here says, "Throw it out."

What? Throw out my reel-to-reel tape recorder, my red knit polyester leisure suit, my lava lamp, and my Time magazine with the picture of the Apollo 11 moon landing on the cover? She's got to be kidding.

But it would be nice to be able to use my desk again.

40-

Twinkles for Your Wrinkles

Remember when everybody was saying, "Never trust anybody over the age of thirty?" Now I hardly know anybody under the age of thirty.

Have you ever noticed that the older you get, the older "old" is? Big Louie always says, "The bad news is that your life just flies by. The good news is that you can usually be the pilot." You learn stuff as you go along, like the best things in life aren't things, almost everything you do that's wonderful, you'll catch hell for, and cookies you eat over the sink have no calories. And putting a red bulb in your bedroom light makes your wrinkles disappear. (Try it.)

I mostly like being a member of the Louie Louie generation. That's because I still have some twinkles in my wrinkles. Wrinkled was not one of the things I wanted to become when I grew up. But it's okay, because I still have several moving parts, which my Lady W. Wench helps me move on a reasonably regular basis.

Louie Louie Generation guys and girls have a big advantage in figuring things out: it's called been there, done that. We know, for example, that one size doesn't fit any. A distant relative has not died and left us a fortune so all we have to do to get it is send our social security number to an Internet guy in Nigeria. And tears get you sympathy, but sweat gets you results.

Big Louie wants us to keep lots of things in perspective. He always says, "The more you know, the more you know you don't know … very much." And he's right. I don't know the answers to many important questions, like how big is the universe, where did my six pack of abs go, and what is the absolute limit to how sexy my Lady Wonder Wench can look.

But you will be proud of me, because I am beginning to understand a little bit about computers. For example, it is never a good idea to let a computer know you're in a hurry. Because every time you do, you get a little screen that says, "We are downloading sixty-five absolutely vital updates. This will take roughly a week, more if you have a slow downloader. Do not turn off your computer—or else." And I also figured out how a computer can answer in a few seconds, mathematical questions that would take you millions of years to work out. You know how they do that? They make the answers up. That's how. They know you're not going to take a million years to check them out.

You can make lots of stuff up when you're a kid. Things are kinda loosey-goosey when you're playing street stickball. But if you grow up and make it to the major leagues, there are umpires who make you play it strictly according to the rules. Of course Louie Louie lads and ladies have also learned that one of the most important rules, is that there are times when you have to have the guts to break the rules, even if that risks having an umpire throw you out of the game.

It's not all cut and dried. There are some things about being a Louie Louie Generation guy that works two ways. Pretty women will flirt with you. And that's nice. But the reason they'll flirt with you is that they feel safe doing it. I'd like them to think there's at least a little danger still lurking in the beast. I carry a picture of my

Lady Wonder Wench and me that was taken at a beach a long time ago. We look… different. That doesn't make me feel old. It makes me feel lucky. The thing I hate is that I have to put on my glasses to see the picture clearly.

Attitude/gratitude. All in all I'm really happy, healthy, hot and comfortable as I'm sitting here in my Louie Louie Generation wrinkles. I hope you're happy, healthy, hot and comfortable in yours too.

41-

Feeling Cape-able

L ouie Louie Generation guys have earned the right to be comfortable. That's why I have just changed from my formal business attire—my black silk and leather cape with the sterling-silver clasps, my gold lamé loincloth, and matching purple ostrich feather, to these jeans, which have, as the commercial says, "A skosh more room." They go nicely with my "Save the Dinosaurs" T-shirt, with the hole under the left armpit, and my purple orthopedic sweat socks. It's not stylish, but it's me. It's comfortable.

Much to my delight, I have found that women like to snuggle with capable, comfortable guys. And like most Louie-Louie Generation guys, I am very capable of giving singularly superior snuggles. Louie Louie guys will smuggle a snuggle into our lives at every opportunity.

And we are capable guys. Think about it. Cape-able. Almost all super heroes slip on their capes when they are about to do super hero stuff: Superman, Batman, Wonder Woman, Zorro. Think about it. The word says it all. The word "cape" means a cape. The word "able" means you can do stuff. So cape-able means you are able to do stuff when you wear your cape. And I've found that's true, even if you're only wearing an imaginary cape like the one I just told you I was just wearing.

Most Louie-Louie Generation guys have good imaginations. And we are comfortable enough about who we are so that even when we're really just wearing our jeans instead of an imaginary cape like the one I was just not really wearing, we don't mind telling our women, "Hey, we're just guys, so don't expect too much of us." Being comfortable with ourselves is just one of our many endearing qualities.

I really did wear a cape once. A real one. It was a long time ago. I was conducting an orchestra for an operetta. What a feeling of power you get when you flip a cape over your shoulders. You feel cape-able. And when you feel cape-able, it's easy to feel comfortable.

The best part of this is that Louie Louie Generation women, like my Lady Wonder Wench, really like to cuddle with a cape-able, comfortable guy, even when the cape is only in his imagination, and he's really just sitting in his big, black, comfortable, leather poppa chair, wearing an old torn T-shirt and slightly smelly sweat socks and jeans. Well…maybe I should change my socks.

42-

Handprints on the Carpet

There are handprints on the carpet again here in front of my big, manly, comfortable, black-leather poppa chair in my living room. The handprints are there because I'm doing push-ups again, which has me feeling pretty good. I had a nasty knee replacement operation a while ago, and it left me a little weak. Push-ups and I go back a long way. I used to do them with my dad when I was a little kid. I always wanted to be like my dad. The push-ups made me into a pretty solid kid, which was good growing up in Brooklyn. The other kids on the block called me "Dick the P. P." I'll give you a politically correct translation: it means Dick the push-up … person. Sort of.

There was no political correctness back then. In those days, a hooker was a hooker, not a "horizontally accessible libido provider." Guys had beer bellies, not "overly developed liquid grain storage organs." And idiots were idiots, not "victims of rectal-cranial inversions." I hate that PC stuff. I don't see anything demeaning about being a female person who acts. We used to call women who did that actresses. Now they're actors. Am I supposed to call my granddaughters "grand-persons?"

Anyway, I was proud of my P. P. nickname, even though I couldn't say it in front of my mother. In fact, I used to sign my name "Dick, P. P." sometimes. Just like some guys put PhD or MD after their names. Those initials kind of followed me into the radio business. While I was in college, I worked evenings at a little station in New Rochelle, and the show I did was called "Platter Poppa." The title was not my idea.

And now … I am once again, Dick Summer, P. P., and the P. P stands for Puma Person. I have declared myself the Grand and Exaulted Poobah of the P. P. A., the Puma People of America. We are Louie Louie Generation folks who are determined to walk and pounce like pumas … again. Here's the point: This knee replacement is a nasty operation … the details of which I will spare you because you don't need nightmares. But just let me say you're supposed to use a walker or crutches or a cane after it … which, of course, I refuse to do.

I fully intend in the very near future, to be ready to pounce like a puma when my Lady wanders into the room wearing something she calls "a little more comfortable." If you're too careful after an operation like that, the old rocking chair will get you. And that's how you get old. You've got to double 'tude it. Pumas never get old. They always have more pounce to the ounce.

Actually … my kids are now older than I feel like I should be. One way I'm going to maintain my Grand and Exaulted Poobah position in the Puma People of America is by avoiding hobble-hood. Which means no more operations. If I develop a constant ringing in my ear, I'll just get an unlisted ear. If my teeth turn yellow, I'll just wear a brown shirt. If my other knee gives out, I'll get a pogo stick.

No hobble hood. Every day, handprints on the carpet. Dick, P.P. Once again, a Puma Person poised to pounce.

43-

Help, I'm Shrinking

I am shrinking. I can't feel it, but I now know for sure that I am shrinking! Isn't that what the Wicked Witch of the West said in The Wizard of Oz? "OOOhhhh … I am shrinking."

As you know, psychiatrists are called "shrinks." And because my age index is pretty high, but my maturity level hasn't kept up with it, I often wonder if "I'm shrinking" is what psychiatrists say when the phone rings while they're working: "I can't talk to you now. Don't you know I have a client here, and I'm busy shrinking?" Can you imagine listening to a shrink dealing with a manic-depressive patient? "Cheer up. Calm down. Cheer up. Calm down." That would wear anybody down. Maybe that's why they call psychiatrists "shrinks." They're all worn down.

I guess a patient who gives a shrink a hard time might be called shrink resistant. I have some shirts that claim to be shrink resistant. That always confuses me. If a shirt is shrink resistant, does that mean that it's not shrink proof, but it really tries hard not to shrink? Obviously, it's bad enough to have a shirt that can't help shrinking, but now I have to contend with the fact that I am shrinking too, and I can't help it.

The irony here is that I was a rather successful competitive swimmer and an ocean lifeguard, so I spent a lot of time in the water. I never had any problems with shrinking before this. And speaking of irony, maybe we should consider the question of whether irony is the opposite of wrinkly. Because besides shrinking, I seem to be getting wrinkly too.

Here's how I found out I'm shrinking: I had an appointment with Dr. Boyd today. Just a regular checkup. Before I saw Dr. Boyd, his new and very pretty nurse had me take off my shoes and stand on the scale. She wanted to check both my weight and my size. So I stood up as tall and straight as I could, just like my mom used to tell me to do. "Stand up straight, Dickie. Respect yourself," she used to say.

But it turned out that no matter how straight I stood, there were two inches less of me than there was back when I was a hunk. Wasn't that just yesterday? It's especially embarrassing for a guy when a woman as pretty as that nurse measures you and tells you you're two inches shorter than you've been claiming to be for years. Shorter in height. Let's be clear.

I like Dr. Boyd, even though he keeps insisting I should have a colonoscopy. I always tell him I'm not sitting still for that. He always gives a chuckle that sounds a little like Clint Eastwood choking on a potato chip, and then he gives me that lecture about polyps and other very disgusting things that they like to find down there where only people with sick minds would think of looking. But he's a good guy, and when he gets finished making me sick telling me about the stuff they find when they poke around inside your bowels, we always tell each other a couple of jokes.

He tells me doctor jokes, and I tell him pilot jokes. He said a patient came in the other day with a cucumber stuck in his right ear, a carrot stuck in his left hear, and a banana up his nose. I bit. I said, "What did you tell him?" He said, "I told him he wasn't eating right."

Then I told him a pilot joke I heard from a flight instructor, who said, "Any landing you can walk away from is a good landing. If you can use the plane again, it's a great landing." We both had a good laugh.

Then he said, "Go stand up against the wall." And he made a pencil mark on the wall at the top of my head. He said, "Go get a colonoscopy, or next time you come in, I'll show you how much you've shrunk since this time." I hate shrinking.

Why am I shrinking? Why are we designed like this? Look at us. Why did God put something as drippy and disgusting as your nose over your mouth? Why didn't He put our ears under our arms? That would keep our ears warm in the winter, and you'd get some exercise, because every time somebody said something, you'd have to lift your elbow and say, "Huh?" Why does hair stop growing on guys' heads and start growing in silly places like our ears? And while I'm complaining about how God set things up for us, how come everything on the planet has to eat the other stuff on the planet to survive? That leads to ideas like life is sacred—but only human life. Look at that cute little lamb. Pow. Lamb chops, anyone? Hey, we have to eat. It doesn't make sense.

Lots of stuff doesn't make sense. How come having sex isn't illegal, but showing pictures of it is? Are we are called homo sapiens because we act like a bunch of saps? I've got to admit we often don't do things you would expect from a species called homo smart-iens. Why do we say silly things to each other? "Drive safely. Be careful. Have a nice day. Have safe sex." Stupid. Doesn't mean anything. When somebody says, "Have a nice day" I always say, "Thanks, but I have other plans."

Back in Brooklyn, when I was a teenager, safe sex meant seeing to it that her parents wouldn't be home until midnight. And by the way, if we were Homo smart-iens, we'd be smart enough to admit that there is no such thing as safe sex. Nothing that powerful is safe.

Part of its power comes from the fact that it's not safe. It's exciting. And dangerous. It's like love. Fall in love and you're risking getting hurt big time, or worse yet, you risk hurting the person you love. Love's not safe. Nothing that powerful is safe.

So, I'm shrinking. I guess most Louie-Louie Generation folks are shrinking. Some of us think that makes us somehow smaller and less significant. But personally, I'm not going to take shrinking lying down. I'm doing something about it. I'm double 'tude-ing this, by remembering Mom's advice. I'm two inches shorter than I used to be. In height. But I'm making up for it by standing up as straight as I can. It's amazing. It works. Try it. Pull your shoulders back, and reach for the sky with the back of your head. It makes you feel like you've just plugged your 'tude into a million-volt socket. It somehow makes you respect yourself again.

I think how much respect we have for ourselves is a much better measurement for who we are than inches anyway.

44-

Clap Hands for Tinker Bell

When I was a very young guy, I met the fairy called Tinker Bell in a book about Peter Pan, and I fell helplessly in love with her. I knew it wasn't going to work out for us because she was in love with Peter—even though she knew there wasn't anything in it for her. She was a fairy, and he was a human. There could never be three bedrooms with a white picket fence around in it for her. And besides, he didn't really care about her. All he wanted from her was her magic fairy dust so he could keep flying, beat up nasty old Captain Hook, and stay young. Like lots of Pimple People guys, he was an immature jerk. But she loved him anyway—even though there wasn't anything in it for her. Nothing.

That's love. Real love. Real magic.

Magic lives. Not the pull-the-rabbit-out-of-the-hat kind. That's not magic, that's just a good trick. When I say, "magic lives," I'm talking about Tinker Bell's kind of magic. There's a huge difference. Trick magic you have to see to believe. Real magic, Tinker Bell's fairy-dust kind, you have to believe first—before you get to see it. Trick magic is great fun. But it's the real magic that keeps you young; it helps you win your battles; sometimes it even makes you able to fly.

Magic works better some times than it does at other times. I don't think it ever dies, but I do think it gets tired and goes to sleep, like Tinker Bell does when she runs out of fairy dust. Of course, maybe Tink doesn't go to sleep. Maybe she just gets scared and hides. Either way, she sometimes looks as if she's in pretty bad shape.

The book said that if we want to keep Tinker Bell alive, we've got to believe in her. And we need to let her know we believe by clapping our hands for her. I think the longer we're around, the more important it is for us to clap our hands for Tink if we don't want to get old and crumbly, if we want to win our battles, and if we want to enjoy an occasional flight. We all need an occasional daily adult dose of fairy dust.

We all need someone to clap hands for us. We all need someone to believe in us. What do you do at a concert, a play, or a ball game? You applaud the performer to let him know you've seen or heard his magic and it's wonderful. You let him know you believe in him. If you didn't applaud, in no time at all, Mick Jagger, Elton John, and Indiana Jones would become just a bunch of worn-out old men dressed up in funny clothes. We all need someone to clap hands for us—even if we happen to be alone in life and that someone who's doing the clapping has to be just ourselves. All by ourselves, we count too.

I can still swing a pretty good softball bat, but these days I'm playing first base instead of center field. And I won't be doing any more pop-up slides. I'm a Louie Louie Generation guy. That means I'm more than a few weeks past my springtime, and there's nothing I can do about that except keep believing in magic—attitude/gratitude—staying happy, healthy and hot. And I like clapping hands for Tinker Bell. That usually, not always, but usually, works for me.

I'm looking at a couple of Captain Hook kind of things that will probably happen to me this coming year, including the probability that I won't be doing my day job anymore. I've been working since

I was thirteen, and it's going to be quite a change. And the fact that I'll be saving gas money by not having to drive to the bank with my paycheck any more somehow isn't making me feel a lot better.

My oldest son David has been pointing out that with some extra time, I'll be able to become the best small-plane pilot at my airport. David's a computer whiz and a musician, who has made a good life for himself and his wife Julie, so he may be on to something. My tall guy son Eric thinks I should finally sit down and write a small library of grown-up bedtime stories. He's a smart guy too. In fact he's an inventor, so I've got to pay attention to what he says too. And our daughter Kris thinks it would be nice if I took a very long vacation with my Lady Wonder Wench. Good idea. We haven't done that in some time.

And speaking of my Lady Wonder Wench, yesterday, when I mentioned being worried about getting old, she smiled, did that silky-legs walk of hers into the bedroom. And a few minutes later, she clapped her hands a few times. So naturally I went in there to see what she was up to. It was Tinker Bell time. She had changed into something she likes to call "a little more comfortable." It was the outfit that I call her two piece: her slippers. She then issued me my minimum adult daily requirement of magic, love, and a supplemental dose of fairy dust.

Magic lives. Tinker Bell sometimes runs out of fairy dust. But like my Lady she knows where it is, and she knows how to get more. And she probably will if she thinks you believe in her.

So I have a simple suggestion for any Louie-Louie lad or lady who is alarmed at the thud of another calendar hitting the floor. If you want to avoid being a youngster in a suddenly obsolete body, wondering what happened, if you want to stay young, learn to fly, and beat up the Captain Hooks in your life, take a chance. Do the double 'tude. Attitude/ gratitude. Stay happy, healthy and hot. And clap hands for Tinker Bell one more time.

What have you got to lose?

45-

Hot and Kool

I like being comfortable. But like anybody else, except for your oh-so-very koolest guys (that's kool with a k), I sometimes get frazzled and furious. I have started fistfights at times. And I have been known to leak suspiciously around the eyes at sad movies or moving music. Very un-kool. And I don't care who knows it.

I am usually a mellow fellow. I like being that kind of cool. But not the kind you spell with a k. I also like getting hot. Getting hot has gotten me into a lot of trouble in my life. It's left me with scars from fights and scars from love affairs, and it's gotten me fired from radio stations and damn near gotten me killed a couple of times trying to do some crazy things that simply couldn't be done—not by me at least. But you know what? It's worth it. It's definitely worth it. Heat is neat. Happy, healthy and hot.

I didn't always see it that way. I grew up in the "big boys don't cry" section of Brooklyn, New York. "The Rules" ruled what kool guys did in Brooklyn. And kool-guy Rule number one was "Be kool if you want to be accepted by the other guys." That's kool with a k. That kind of kool meant that all jokes had to have cutting edges. Beauty was something only "chicks" cared about. Fear was for wussies—and so was anything that had to do with a hurting heart. Brooklyn guys weren't supposed to have hearts. We were supposed to be kool. It was as if we were all supposed to grow up and become killers, con-men, or political talk show hosts. Except in my house. My dad was the strongest guy on the block. And the smartest. He always said, "Big boys don't cry, but big men sometimes do. And they don't care who knows it." But of course, he was just Dad. He was old. I was young. What did he know?

Then I had a son—David. There's nothing like having a kid to smack a guy on the side of the head. David taught me a huge lesson his first day home from the hospital. He was a happy, healthy, tiny, stinky winner, who smiled, waved his arms around, laughed and cried any time he felt like it. He was definitely uncool. And he was wonderful. He still is. No way would I would have wanted to change a thing about any of my kids except maybe their diapers. What a smack on the side of the head. The rule of "the kool Rules" had come to an instant, screeching, laughing, stinky, waving, happy end when David came into my life.

The smacks on the side of the head came hard and fast after that. And each smack seemed to wake up some new part of my brain and open my eyes a little wider. And you should have seen the size of my eyes, when I met my Lady Wonder Wench.

She was tall, elegant, soft-eyed, gentle, funny, and smart. She wasn't kool. Although some guys who tried to get too physical with her accused her of being cold, she wasn't kool and I'm here to tell you, and them, that she certainly wasn't cold. When I met her, she was writing a novel that turned out to be quite successful. It's called, "Love's Forbidden Flame." And she lived by the rules that she wrote about in the wonderful, passionate, fantasy land that she created in her story. She lit my limbic system big time.

But it was a difficult time in our lives, and my impulse was to run away and hide behind the old Brooklyn kool-guy Rules. But I couldn't run. I couldn't even move. She stopped me by just standing close to me and looking up into my eyes, and laughing her warm laugh at my jokes. Even when I finally said, "I have to leave you," she simply said, "Whatever you want." The last thing I wanted to do was to leave her. And eventually, I didn't.

That's when I started writing the stories that became the "lovin' touch" books. It was a learning curve…breaking the Brooklyn kool-guy Rules. But the more often I broke them, the easier it got for me to make my own rules. I definitely wasn't being kool writing about things like love and hurt and passion. But there was a terrible heat building up inside, and writing about it was the only way I could think of to relieve at least some of the pressure. It worked, but only a little, and only for a little while. It eventually blew my life apart. And I had to figure out my own rules to run my new life.

You'll find some of them in this book.

I'm a pilot, and there have been times when an in-flight emergency has made it necessary for me to be cool. But that's cool with a "c," as in "control." That's fine. And I'm pretty good at that. But kool with a k is just a twenty-first-century update on those old Brooklyn kool-guy Rules. And I'm not having any part of that any more.

46-

Big Louie's Top Twenty Tips

What makes a Louie Louie Generation guy the bedmate of choice for so many supermodels and other beautiful and successful women? I've told you that it's our gentlemanly charm, our poise and grace, and the fact that some of us have a little money. But let me give some of you young guys the top twenty list of specific things you can do to help you in your struggle to achieve full-fledged Louie-Louie Guy-hood.

20. If you're going to wear a baseball cap, unless you are an actual catcher in full uniform and the game is still going on, wear your cap peak front like a human.

19. Unless you have religious reasons for wearing your cap indoors, take it off when you walk into a restaurant with a lady.

18. You don't necessarily have to wear a jacket and tie, but don't show up looking like either Barney Rubble or an Elton John impersonator who was left out in the rain overnight.

17. And speaking of adornment, earrings look lovely on the ladies. Especially the dangle ones. But earrings make you look like the pirates of the Carribean just voted you off the island.

16. When a lady trusts you enough to grace your presence in a car, open the door for her and help her in.

15. Then when you get where you're going, reverse the process. Jump out of the driver's seat, open the door, and help her out. Be ready to catch her if she faints from the shock.

14. When you're on a date, do not take cell phone calls. And do not make outgoing cell phone calls either. Some guys think that making calls on a date makes them look important. It doesn't. It makes them look like idiots.

13. Ditch your favorite lines, lies, and general BS. Ladies are smart, and honesty is a lady turn-on.

12. Read a paper or magazine that has nothing to do with your favorite sports team so you have something that has nothing to do with spikes, sneakers, or cleats to talk about with her.

11. Brush your teeth. Or, if you are a hockey goalie, be sure your teeth are properly installed and turned in the right direction.

10. Take a shower and change your socks and underwear. Contrary to what your buddies may tell you, sweat is not a turn-on to most ladies.

9. One or two beers is probably okay. More than that and you are over the lady limit.

8. Show up for the date on time according to whatever actual time zone you were in when you made the date.

7. Shut up and listen to what the lady is saying. Try to understand not only the words, but how she feels about what she's telling you. If she's upset because her cat died, even if you're kinda' glad because the damn cat was a drag, she's not glad, so be genuinely not glad with her.

6. You won't understand everything she says, but there are three key words here: listen, feel, and genuine. Keep them in mind at all times.

5. When out with a lady, keep your fingers and your eyes off other hotties.

4. Do not sit in your car and blow your horn for her. Ring the bell, smile, and escort her to the car.

3. Bring her some small surprise. Doesn't have to be a dozen roses, a dandelion you picked from the lawn is fine.

2. She has done something to make herself look especially pretty for you. Figure out what it is and compliment her on it.

1. Always protect her. Job number one. Make her feel safe, relaxed, and beautiful.

Do these things. Make Big Louie proud.

47-

Big Louie Says, "Don't Say This Stuff"

Here are the twenty things Big Louie says a Louie Louie Generation Guy in training shouldn't ever say to a woman:

20. "Don't worry about it. It's no big deal." Right. I know it's hard not to say that, because they worry about all kinds of things, like "Are you using the right salad fork?" "Is that sound your socks scrunching?" "We're going to be late for the ballet." But stifle yourself. A closed mouth gathers no feet.

19. "I'm sorry, now let's just forget it." Come on, unless you've shouted the wrong name in a moment of passion, how long should you have to beg, plead, and wheedle for forgiveness? But they're not going to buy it. So suffer in manly silence.

18. "And to think I was really trying to pick up your friend." No matter how warm and fuzzy you're feeling, lying there by the fireplace or wherever, if you say anything like that, you are doomed. There is no hope.

17. "If you're not happy, there's nothing I can do about it." That's dumb too. Because if you can't do anything about it, some other guy will.

16. "Don't be ridiculous, of course I love you." Never go there, guys. Never. If she's worried you may not love her, you're making her feel weak instead of strong. And that makes you a jerk.

15. "My God, will you get to the point?" My Lady Wonder Wench put that one away for me when we were first going out. She said, "I only talk too much when I'm happy." What was I supposed to say, "Don't be happy"?

14. "From now on, I'll handle everything." No. After saying that you'll handle nothing from now on.

13. "What do you mean, I don't listen. I can tell you everything you just said." It's not a pop quiz, guys. She doesn't mean you didn't listen to her. She meant you didn't hear her. Big difference.

12. "Your friend Mary is really built." That kind of comment is what causes the Lorena Bobbit Syndrome in which women alter guys' anatomy with scissors.

11. "Don't talk about it, just do it." Guys, talking about it is part of how women get things done. In fact, sometimes if they talk about it enough, we do it for them.

10. "Be glad I remembered to put the toilet seat up." That makes sense only until the first time you sit down by mistake while the seat is up. It's not a great experience.

9. "Why can't I? Your cousin always lets me do that." You have now finished yourself with both your girl and her cousin—and any other female within a fifty-mile radius of your zip code.

8. "You're a typical woman." There is no such thing as a typical woman. There are typical men but no typical women. And if you don't know that, you have no hope for reproduction.

7. "You're just like your mother." That's just a low blow—for both women. And you only get one blow that low per romance before it turns into just a relationship.

6. "How old are you?" The only exception to the don't-say-how-old-are-you rule is when you're a little concerned that she may be under eighteen.

5. "I'll call you." Either don't say it, just do it, or just don't say it.

4. "I don't want to talk about it." Now that's just dumb. And you are about to experience one of the most awful forces of mother nature, the dreaded silent treatment.

3. "I'm busy." She is the most important part of your busy, or she should be.

2. "I know exactly how to get where we're going." Whoops. One wrong turn, guys, and you get to star in your own personal head-on collision with a diesel-powered "I told you so."

And here it is. The number one thing a man should never say to a woman. This is unnecessary. No Louie Louie lad would ever say a thing like this, would he? I guess maybe so. Anyway, here it is.

1. Never make any positive statement that ends with the word "but." As in "I love you, but …"

That's not to be confused with the similar sounding, but totally different statement, "I love your butt." Under some circumstances, that one's okay.

48-

Big Louie's Ten Happy Helpers

Sometimes you've got to work at being happy so you can be healthy and hot. So Big Louie has a genuine list of 10 Happiness Helpers for you if you're feeling kind of down and droopy today.

#10- Listen to some happy music. That's pretty simple #9- Get up and move around a little more. When you move, you groove. #8- Stand and sit tall, and walk strong. Stop the slouch. Pull your shoulders back and reach for the sky with the back of your head. This really works. When you walk tall and strong, you look at life differently. Walk strong, like you're going somewhere. Strut, don't wander or mosey. Try it. People get out of your way. And you start disturbing the hormones of all those whose hormones you want to disturb for miles around. #7- Fake it till you feel it. Put a smile on your face…it'll actually make you feel smiley. #6- Hang with happy people as much as you can. #5- Drink lots of cold water. Seriously. I've tried it. Give it a shot. #4- Take up as much space as possible. Spread out. Do stuff like draping your arms out across the back of the couch. #3- Walk into your clothes closet where nobody can hear you and holler whatever is ticking you off out loud. #2- Go find a picture of yourself that was taken at a happy time, and put it somewhere you have to see it every day. Or make up a happy hero story about yourself, and add to it every day. #1- Do at least one small thing for yourself... just for yourself every day. Or if you don't feel like doing any of those things...don't. But give this one Happy Helper a quick try. Just take five very deep breaths...all the way down to the bottom of your belly.

It'll warm up and stir your personal juices. Happy, healthy and hot.

49-

Rock and Roll Is Here to Stay

I'm sitting here in my big, manly, comfortable, black-leather poppa chair in my living room—which is good, because I got an e-mail a little while ago with some news that would have knocked me down if I weren't already sitting. When I finished reading it and I called my Lady Wonder Wench to tell her about it she said something that sounded like "Oh my God, wow." I think she was holding her cell phone at arm's length as she got to the word wow. I only think that's what she said, because the last word came out on a note that was so high and loud that I couldn't really hear it, but golden retrievers for three blocks around fled in terror, and windows and eyeglasses cracked all over the zip code.

It was great news, but it really screwed up my day, because I completely forgot about everything else, including the fact that I was supposed to be interviewed on a radio program about my books and CDs. Forgetting things like that was not only unprofessional, it was simply inconsiderate and impolite. I'm a Louie Louie Generation guy. Louie Louie Generation guys have manners.

I guess I should tell you about the e-mail that knocked me down. I feel kind of funny about it. But if I don't tell you, you'll probably hear about it anyway, because the folks who sent the e-mail say they plan on doing quite a bit of publicity.

The note says, in part, "Dear Dick Summer, the museum has just unveiled a complete redesign that tells the story of rock and roll in a more linear fashion. We have updated all museum technology to state-of-the-art, including the interactive kiosks. You, and your impact on rock music, are featured in the new exhibit." Signed, Margaret Thresher, Director of Communications, Rock and Roll Hall of Fame Museum.

Oh my God, WOW!

50-

Memory Mirrors

U sually when I'm looking in a mirror, it's just a glance while I'm shaving or combing my hair. I used to look in the mirror while I was tying my tie, but I very seldom do that anymore. Thankfully, suits and ties are mostly in my past now. I look so much better these days dressed casually in my Pierre Cardin gold lamé loincloth with the matching Lands End purple ostrich feather. My Lady Wonder Wench says the glitter on the eyelids is a little "uptown," so I only wear that to meetings with clients.

If you stare into a full-length mirror long enough, it starts working like a crystal ball that's running backward. It'll make you stand up straighter and suck your belly in. And that starts the projector going on lots of memory movies.

Most of my memory movies have happy endings. One of them starts out with a shot of Dick "the college kid" Summer, standing in the lobby of the RCA Building in New York, greeting visitors to the NBC Radio and TV studios. Marble floor. Eight hours. But the college kid can take it with a constant smile. The sound track goes something like this:

"Good afternoon, Mr. Steve Allen. Good evening, Mr. Chet Huntley." And, of course, the occasional, "Sorry, sir, you need an NBC pass to use that elevator." That last comment was about the extent of "security" at NBC in those days.

Fast forward a few years, and zoom in on the face in my full-length mirror movie: It's young and excited and trying to look nonchalant, walking into that same lobby. The college kid at the velvet rope smiles and says, "Good evening, Mr. Dick Summer." Music comes in right about there, chasing the chill that still runs up my spine when I think about it.

Eventually, while I was on the air at WNBC in New York, the college kid at the velvet rope in the lobby was joined by members of the crack NBC security system at night. They were not exactly Navy Seal-type guards. Mostly, they were guys from Brooklyn, Staten Island, Queens, or the Bronx, working for some extra bucks to pay the rent or send a kid to college. Nice, hard-working, New York kind of guys, usually tired after their day jobs and certainly not the kind of highly trained, motivated killers you would want on ready alert to defend with their lives whoever was upstairs working the overnight hours on radio or TV. It sometimes seemed their main function was to stop my Lady Wonder Wench, or any other family members or friends, from coming up to the second-floor radio studio without permission from the guy on the air. Me.

As I said, security was far from airtight. One morning at around 4:30 a.m., I had the feeling someone was watching. I looked up, and sure enough, there was a guy standing outside the studio glass where the tours go during the day, and he was watching Vic Lombardo, my engineer, and me do the show. Actually, we were eating lunch during a tape playback of a previous night's show, which is what usually happened most nights from 4:00 to 5:00 a.m. But I'm pretty sure we looked like we were working. Between 4:00 and 5:00 a.m., there's very little difference between how guys look when they're working and when they're eating their lunch anyway.

I didn't think that was too strange, because the Tom Snyder TV Show offices were just down the hall, and I figured it was just some staff guy working late. But a few minutes later, he walked slowly into the studio, seriously disrupting my enjoyment of my ham and Swiss on rye and Vic's cold coffee and Playboy magazine.

Instantly my finely honed NBC page training kicked in, and I said, "Sorry, sir, but you can't come in here without an NBC pass."

Vic, not having the benefit of that same sophisticated training, was more blunt. I think he said something like "Yeah, wadda you want?"

The guy's eyes got wide, and he started to shake. He said, "Please don't tell the doctors I'm here." We didn't inform the doctors, but Vic took him by one arm and I took him by the other, and we put him back on the elevator, hit "Lobby" and went back to the studio and locked the door so we could finish lunch.

Some people, however, never had any trouble getting past security. They were a group of young women I came to call the "midtown-Manhattan ladies." As those of you who are familiar with Manhattan know, the NBC studios are right in the middle of just about everything: right across from Radio City Music Hall and only a block or so away from the best clubs in town. Some of the young ladies who worked at those clubs often sought refuge, and perhaps some other human solace, in other "open all night" venues—like the NBC studios.

As I said, the security guys weren't ex-Navy Seals. They were tired guys who figured that there's nothing like a middle-of-the-night visit from one of these scantily clad maidens to wake up the guys upstairs on the overnight shift. And they were right. (There is a need to be careful of graphic descriptions here due to the Lady Wonder Wench factor, among other considerations.) But suffice it to say, it was not unusual for a lady in a raincoat, a smile, and little else to slip past security and find her way up to the studio. I was delighted.

I'll never forget the first time one showed up. Very pretty. Slim. Long, dark hair. Soft, gravelly voice. Probably twenty-two. She walked over to where I was sitting, smiled, and reached down to give me a kiss on the cheek as she told me how wonderful my show was. In the process, one of her several charms became stunningly obvious as it slipped out from under her only half-buttoned raincoat.

Now here's where it gets weird. Hormones came humming into my brain at exactly the same time that a picture of my Lady Wonder Wench popped up right behind my vibrating eyes. I don't need to tell you about the humming hormones, but the picture of my Lady Wonder Wench deserves a description. She wasn't angry, just hurt, like I'd never seen her hurt. It was just an instant picture, but it absolutely cancelled out the hormones, and they immediately stopped sending signals to the hands to which they were attached.

It was a sharp slap on the side of the head. And from then on, incredibly, I started treating the midtown-Manhattan ladies more politely than passionately. Now, I like ladies—especially lustful, half-clad ladies in the middle of the night. It wasn't a matter of "being faithful," being afraid of getting caught, or being afraid of sinning or any of that stuff. It was just a simple, straightforward shot to the gut that I have never forgotten. I don't ever want to see my Lady Wonder Wench hurt like that. Not ever. The experience turned off my testosterone. I never thought it would happen to me.

It became like one of those old black-and-white movies with people like Lauren Bacall and Ingrid Bergman and Cary Grant, I guess. It's a story that's been told over and over again, the story of the ladies who come and go in the lives of guys who work in the night.

But on the outside chance that one of those "midtown-Manhattan ladies" might be reading this, no, I am not gay; yes, you were absolutely stunning. And I was fascinated and delighted to see you—almost all of you, for that matter. And no, I'll never forget you. But it was just the wrong time and the wrong place in my life for anything more than simply remembering how you starred in one of my memory movies.

51-

Witchy Woman

I got to know a cigar-smoking, truck-driving, witchy woman at WNBC. Man, what a woman. Her real name is Lisa, but her friends call her Olga. Olga the Witch has long black hair, a voice like a purr with fur, and a long slow-motion smile. I didn't see Olga walk into the studio. I just looked up, and she was suddenly standing there in studio 2b at WNBC Radio a lot of years ago. The idea that she just "appeared" was probably just my imagination. Maybe.

The 10:00 p.m. to midnight portion of my show was music, and midnight to 2:00 a.m. was talk. I always liked to have ordinary people who did extraordinary things as guests on the talk portion. So just before Halloween, I asked for mail from folks who figured they qualified, and Olga's note said, "I'm a witch." It was a slam dunk.

The lights at the WNBC studios were New York neon, and Olga purred something about how comfortable we'd be if I turned off the overheads and did our interview by the light of a candle she'd brought. Olga worked well in the dark with just a candle. She liked candlelight; it was enough light so you could just see a person's face and especially a person's eyes. If it weren't for the Federal Disc Jockey

Act's regulations, plus the fact that my crack NBC tech/accomplice Vic Lombardo was only one heavy-breath away—and, of course, the certain knowledge that my Lady Wonder Wench was listening—things could have gotten a little out of hand right there.

Olga was fascinating. I mean in other ways, too. She was a follower of the ancient pagan religion called Wicca. It's about love of nature, gentleness toward humans and animals, and very ancient legends about tall trees, shadow creatures, and the moon. No devil worship, no broomsticks, and no haggle-tooth hags. Olga was beautiful, smart, sensitive, and loyal. I invited her back for several shows and eventually got to know her pretty well. As a matter of fact, she became a real friend to my Lady Wonder Wench, our son Mark, and me.

Mark was fourteen when Olga came into our lives. He often came to the station with my Lady Wonder Wench and me on Friday nights. Friday nights were "Mouth vs. Ear" nights on my show. "Mouth vs. Ear" was a quiz show. We always won, because we cheated. It was a lot of fun.

On Olga's first night as a member of the Mouth quiz-show team, she was lively, happy, and braless. And that's how she threw her arms around Mark and gave him a loud, juicy, bouncy kiss smack dab on the mouth.

Mark was big with the girls at fourten. But Olga was all woman. Mark's ears wiggled, his hands stuck out from his arms at a strange angle, and I think he didn't start breathing again until sometime late Saturday afternoon.

That was lots of years ago, but when I asked Mark yesterday if he remembered, he said something like "Oooooh yessss." And his eyes turned a little purple.

Olga fell in love and moved away with her guy a few years ago. I wonder if you might know her. I don't want to give you her last name, for obvious reasons. But that wouldn't be necessary anyway.

Because there's only one Olga like this warm and wonderful witchy woman. If you know her, I'd appreciate it if you'd ask her to drop an e-mail to dick@dicksummer.com. Lady Wonder Wench, Mark, and I really miss that cigar-smoking, truck-driving, fur-purring, witchy woman.

52-

Imus in the Morning

There are at least two Don Imus-es. One was the rowdy drunk and pothead who worked at WNBC. The other was the cowboy and political kingmaker you hear today. Fortunately for both, there is Charles McCord. It's not true that Charles is the brain in the Imus machine. But he contributes much more than anybody realizes to the success of the guy you hear on the air. I like Charles a lot. He's a gentleman and a very smart guy. I also like Imus—the Imus who dried out and got to work on time. Not that other guy.

Don came as close as anybody I ever worked with to finding his teeth on the floor one morning when he wandered in more than an hour late. I had been on the air since my show started at 10:00 p.m. the night before. The 2:00 a.m. to 6:00 a.m. guy had been fired, and I was filling in until they hired someone else. So I was doing morning drive after being on the air for eight hours. Don's technician wasn't going to go out of his way to help anybody sound good doing Don's show. Details aren't important, but Don really got my Brooklyn juices boiling that morning.

Imus did a take-off on my lovin touch stories pretty regularly, and I got a kick out of that. But he was a real pain in the tail before he dried out. A telling Imus quote was heard while the staff was having dinner at an Atlantic City remote: "It's getting very tiring carrying the whole station on my shoulders."

The other Don Imus was a genuinely nice guy. He had a TV show for a while, and even after the bad blood almost got spilled between us, or maybe because of it, he invited me on to talk about and promote my hypnotherapy practice. Anybody who can recover from the alcohol/drug dependency that had Don in its grip has my admiration.

The transformation of his show into a genuine political force is mind-boggling. But even more astonishing is the transformation from the foul-mouth roughneck to the good-guy husband and father he is today. Don's a special guy, and I'm delighted at his success and wish him many more years at the top of his trade.

53-

The Night Bird Purrs

Allison Steele called herself The Night Bird. Allison did overnights when I did mornings on WNEW-FM. She looked just like she sounded: smoky, smooth, and sexy. She wore short leather skirts very, very well. She had a wicked, slow smile and a big, soft, gentle heart in a nicely curved sweater, and as I said, a very short leather skirt. Did I mention a very short leather skirt?

She was a stunning example of a Louie Louie lady. She left a little trace of perfume and a couple of kind words everywhere she went. Allison was inducted into the Rock and Roll Hall of Fame long before I was represented there, but she never talked about that. She liked talking to men, and I liked that. We enjoyed a cup of coffee together every morning for a while—my first and her last of the day. She also liked talking about men. Amazingly, Allison and my Lady Wonder Wench got together at a party one evening, and they formed an instant female friendship. They spent a remarkable part of the night talking about me. My Lady Wonder Wench wouldn't discuss most of the conversation except to say that there was a lot of laughing and a little sneaky finger-pointing involved.

Allison single-handedly saved half the stray cats in Manhattan from destruction. She took them in, nursed them back to health, and found homes for them. Allison was one of the funniest, warmest, classiest women I've ever known. And certainly one of the sexiest. She really enjoyed being a girl.

"The flutter of wings, the sounds of the night, the shadow across the moon, as the Nightbird lifts her wings and soars above the earth into another level of comprehension where we exist only to feel. Come fly with me, Alison Steele, the Nightbird." That was her show open. For almost twenty years, her purr warmed New Yorkers' ears—and possibly some other body parts. If you're a Jimi Hendrix fan, you may remember the song he wrote for her. It's called "Night Bird Flying."

She left us, way too soon, on September 27, 1995. Allison was about fun, fur, and female sex. Kinda hard to find that kind of sex on the radio these days—or these nights—sex, not porn.

I think the difference between sexy and pornographic is simple. Sexy looks/sounds/feels like both people are having fun. Pornographic looks/sounds/feels like somebody's getting hurt. I respect what Howard Stern does, and I certainly respect the size of his paycheck. I don't listen to him or any of his wannabees anymore, but when I have heard them, it always sounded to me like the guys were having much more fun than the ladies who were involved.

There was a wonderful, powerful woman behind that Night Bird purr. I know Howard. He used to do an occasional Dick Summer imitation for fun. We had the same agent, Don Buchwald. Howard was way too smart to ever invite somebody like Allison to be on his show. She'd have laughed that soft, sexy laugh and sent him to his room, alone.

Allison was one of the funniest, warmest, classiest women I ever met. And that's the witchcraft that leaked out of the magic radio box when she died. It was a warm and gentle love potion—

powerful, female fun. A little trace of perfume and a couple of kind words. And class. That's the way it is with Louie Louie Ladies like Allison.

Lots of class.

54-

Wolfie and Me

E very once in a while, I miss sitting in a radio studio late at night—with just a mic, a couple of turntables, and the tech on duty ... On the air at WNBC in the middle of the otherwise-dark skyscraper called the RCA Building in New York, I huddled down with good people who were listening all across America—all of us just trying to make it through the night. Besides the sometimes pretty intense connection with the listeners in the wee small hours, I got to work with some very special folks. Wolfman Jack, for instance.

Yes, that's what he really liked to be called by the other guys at the station. His real name was Bob Smith, and like Cousin Brucie and me, he grew up in Brooklyn. Wolfie was a comic-book character with a huge heart. What most people didn't realize was that the screaming and wolfin' while the mic was open was his act. The quiet shuffling through his liner cards and sometimes singing along while the records played was more like the very likeable guy he really was. (Yes we played records on the air in those days.)

My Lady Wonder Wench came with me to the station frequently, partly just because I liked having her with me and partly to "protect me" from the soft, sweet voices on the request line. That's part of another story I'll tell you some time. But the thing she still says about Wolfie is "He was always a gentleman to me. He was very comfortable." I'd say basically the same thing about him. He was a very comfortable Louie Louie lad.

That's not to say that he didn't know how to howl when the moon was full. As a matter fact, the phase of the moon didn't really have much to do with it when the music got to Wolfie, especially low-down R&B music. Race music is what they used to call it before the great Alan Freed made it mainstream. Wolfie was a black man in white skin; a white man who could definitely jump. And nothing was safe from getting knocked over in the studio when Wolfie was up and jumping.

Sometimes, especially after he had been naughty, things were kind of quiet while the records were playing. I mentioned liner cards, and those of you in the business probably thought it was a misprint. Liner cards are usually station position statements that a program director wants the guy on the air to read at predetermined times. Real interesting stuff like "More music, less talk." That kind of crap. Wolfie's liner cards were different. They contained what he called his "statements to my honeys." Sometimes, quick snippets of philosophy—kind of like the stuff in Jonathan Livingston Seagull. Sometimes, just barely disguised pick-up lines. Sometimes, the words really didn't make much sense at all, except when Wolfie was saying them.

When Wolfie came to WNBC, "Cousin Brucie Morrow" was still at WABC. The WNBC promotion department took a series of ads featuring tombstones with Cousin Brucie's name on it and captions that said something to the effect that Wolfie was here, and Cousin Brucie's time had come. That never happened. And ironically, when Wolfie left WNBC, Cousin Brucie came over to our side.

Wolfie made his radio reputation on the West Coast and over the border in Mexico. But if you ever wonder where he kept his heart, look at the call letters on the microphone in almost all his pictures. They read WNBC, New York. He was a Brooklyn kid who refused to grow up, a genuine Louie-Louie Lad.

I always liked being on the air at night. I called the listeners, "my huddle." That's because, to me, it felt like a football team in a huddle. A bunch of folks protecting and helping each other to make it to the goal, which, in our case, was dawn and a new day. That was something...sitting there in the middle of a dark skyscraper, talking to the world through the tough hours of the night. There were other studios in the middle of the night, one in Boston and one in Indianapolis that I'll never forget. I loved calling the plays for the folks in all my huddles. But Brooklyn was always our home town— Wolfie and me.

55-

Your Cousin and Mine

"Cousin Brucie" Morrow, in person, is exactly as he is on the air: a whirlwind mouth, a nice guy, and a shrewd businessman. Bruce hired on at WNBC after a stunning career at WABC. I don't think I ever saw him in the studio without a phone stuck in each ear, a yellow pad with lots of scribbles on it, and a cup of coffee. Bruce is from Brooklyn, and he's an almost stereotypical wheeler and dealer. He is also an accomplished photographer. I have one of his pictures up on my office wall. Bruce is a sophisticated and cultured man who made it his business to be closely involved with the artists whose records he played, even though many of them were young enough to be his kids. It was his job to hang out with the Beatles, Johnny Maestro and The Brooklyn Bridge, and Dion and the Belmonts. He went very far out of his way to do his job well.

Bruce manufactured his voice. He used it to get attention, which is something an air personality was supposed to do in those days. I don't think he was particularly clever or funny. But there was a genuine personal warmth about the guy that made it into the mic. And that wasn't just an on-air act. Bruce was one of the victims of the famous "Pittman Purge," along with Don Imus, Bob Vernon,

Oogie Pringle, Joe McCoy, and yours truly. Bob Pittman was the new, young program director who had been brought in to turn WNBC into a top-forty radio station. He later went on to be one of the founders of MTV and a very big-time radio executive.

Because I was on the air following Bruce, I was in the studio during his last show on WNBC. The phone was melting off the control board with calls from fans and people in the business. Bruce put lots of them on the air, which didn't sit well with the NBC GRR (Guys Running Radio). I guess they thought people wouldn't have noticed the difference between Cousin Brucie and the new guy they brought in to take over his time slot if Bruce hadn't called attention to the change. They were wrong.

Bruce always did a show. His replacement did an air shift. There is a difference, and New Yorkers knew it. Bruce had an energy about him that made a room light up when he walked in. And when he smiled, stuck out his hand to shake yours, and said hello, you really did get the feeling that you were talking to a cousin. In fact, I'm pretty sure that if I ran into him on the street today, we'd stop in some place and have a couple of beers, a pepperoni pizza and a very warm and happy family reunion.

56-

The Man Who Said No

I really loved being on the radio. Those were the days, and nights, when I first ran into Big Louie. His theme song, Louie Louie was the star of most of the record hops in those days. Any time the party got dull, it was Louie to the rescue. But there was another kind of music born in the sixties. Its mommy was the blues, and its daddy was rock and roll, and the people in power said it was conceived in sin. It was music on fire. Hendrix, Morrison, Clapton. When I heard it for the first time it took me a week to get my eyes closed. Today, you'd call it Classic Rock. And there's something you don't know about it and you should. You don't know about the man who got that music on the air. His name was Al Heacock. And he was a man in the best sense of the word. I know the story because I was privileged to work for Al, and he was my friend.

Once upon a time…all the way back in the sixties…AM radio was still king. Big 50,000 watt flame throwers like WBZ in Boston, WABC in New York, WLS in Chicago, and KFI in Los Angeles ruled. Almost all of them were built on tight top forty foundations. In fact, the play list at WABC was frequently more like the top twenty, with the emphasis on the top three. "All Hits All The Time." Jingle, jangle, jingle. The format was the gospel. Except at Boston's WBZ. This is something that most radio professionals won't believe, but it's true. WBZ never had a format in those days. The guys on the air played whatever we wanted to play, including records from our own personal collections, and tapes from local artists. And in between every single record/tape, we had fun. Oh we had fun. And people loved it.

Today's top radio stations pull around a ten rating in a major market. WBZ consistently pulled north of a twenty five. The mouths at WBZ belonged to Carl deSuze, Dave Maynard, Jay Dunn, Jeff Kaye (and later Ron Landry) Bob Kennedy Bruce Bradley and me. But the brains, and a lot of the heart of the station belonged to the Program Director, Al Heacock.

Al was smart. He was a quiet guy who made a lot of money in the stock market. But he really didn't care about the stock market. Al cared about his radio station, WBZ. It was a station with "tude." When we broadcast from our mobile studio, which was most of the time, we proudly wore our station blazers. It wasn't unusual at all for one of us to drop in on somebody else's show and kibitz for a while. When you walked down the beach, you didn't need to bring your own radio, because everybody around you would have 'BZ turned on and turned up to stun. If you stopped your car for a red light, you'd almost always hear 'BZ coming out of the speaker in the car stopped next to you. Those were the days before cars had air conditioning. The Pimple People wouldn't remember.

For those of you who never heard the station, and for those of you who work in radio and are curious about the legend that was WBZ, here's how Al programmed his music: Each month there was a staff meeting. At the meeting he would always remind us to play some of the top tunes he left in the rack in the studio each week. And then he'd say, "I don't want to hear two records back to back. We pay you guys to entertain. Entertain." What a joy it was, what an honor to be one of Al's guys on WBZ.

Here's what that means to you. If it weren't for Al Heacock, a man who knew how to say no…and stick to his guns…Classic Rock might never have been born. At least it would have been a much longer labor and birth.

Boston has always had a strong Folk Music tradition. At WBZ we were consistently playing original tapes of unreleased songs like "Sounds of Silence" by Simon and Garfunkel, and "The Urge for Going" by Tom Rush, all kinds of stuff by Dylan, and Baez, and Sweet Judy Blue Eyes Collins. I was doing a weekly MC gig at the Unicorn Coffee House, a major Folkie spot in town. And I noticed that some of the artists were beginning to go electric. I invited Al to attend one night, and he got it. Right away. The next day, he instigated 'BZs only mandatory music rule: "One 'Liquid Rock' song per hour." Al called the music Liquid Rock. Almost immediately the new music picked up a different name, "Underground Rock." The name was the only thing Al got wrong.

He gave me two hours on Sunday evenings for the first big time "Underground Rock" radio show. He called it, "Dick Summer's Subway." "Subway" as in "Underground." Then Dylan went electric, Eric Clapton formed "Cream" and Woodstock forged a new musical and political conscience for America, and it went roaring out on WBZ's 50,000 watt clear channel signal all the way from Massachusetts to Midway Island in the Pacific. (I have an air check.)

The suits who owned Group W Radio in New York were aghast. It wasn't top forty. It wasn't anything they recognized. They didn't like it. They wanted it stopped…right now. Al just very quietly said no. For a while, even the suits didn't want to mess too much with Al's 25 rating in Boston. Then Arlo Guthrie did a song called "Alice's Restaurant," featuring a line about the "mother rapers and the father rapers on the Group W bench." The lawyers at Group W headquarters in New York and D.C. freaked.

The President of the Group took a flight from New York to talk sense into this crazy program director Heacock. "Get it off the air now" was the order. Al very quietly said "no." It was a classic Big Suit vs. Radio Guy. And Mr. Suit blinked. The order was changed to "well at least edit that line out" Al very quietly just said "no." If you're a radio professional, you'll realize how far out of line that was. A Program Director is a middle management guy. He was talking to the President of the group.

So Mr. Suit decided to drop in on me personally one Sunday night, "for a friendly visit." The engineer saw what was going on, and called Al to alert him to the situation. Ten minutes later, Al was at the studio. He asked Mr. Suit to join him for a quick meeting...out of the studio. That's the last I heard of the problem.

A few months later, the great Tom Donahue climbed on "Underground" music on his FM station out in San Francisco, Classical Music WBCN went FM rock in Boston, "The Professor," Scott Muni, Rosco, Jon Schwartz and crew took WNEW-FM rock in New York, and invited me to join them, which I did. And in a little while, FM killed the AM king. It probably would have happened anyway. But the point is that when you hear "Smoke on the Water", or "Bohemian Rhapsody" or "Light My Fire" you're listening to some of the many echos of that quiet but firm "no" that Al Heacock said all those years ago.

Al died a while ago. I think it would be appropriate if you'd remember him, the next time you find yourself listening to "Stairway To Heaven."

57-

Twinkle Twinkle Little Star, How I Wonder What You Are

I was sitting here in my big, manly, comfortable black leather poppa chair in my living room listening to our little 3 year old Cecelia sing, when the news about Neil Armstrong's death came in. The song she was singing was a three year old's happy, but very careful version of "Twinkle Twinkle Little Star, How I Wonder What You Are." It was the absolutely perfect song for the occasion. Cecelia is only 3, but she sometimes amazes us with the things she wonders about. Most of the time she's a bundle of bounces and non-stop noise. But I've seen her sit very quietly on our daughter Kris' lap on a Summer evening, and look up at the stars…and wonder… really wonder…what they are.

Neil Armstrong, the first man on the moon, was only a little older than our Cecelia when he had his first plane ride. He was a little kid sitting in a small plane. That ride lit the fuse on a life long rocket ride into history. When the plane ride was over, he told his parents and all his friends, "Guess what! I'm going to be a pilot." When he got a little older he became what we call an airport rat. He got a job fueling and washing airplanes in exchange for flying lessons. And in fact, he got his pilot's license before his driver's license. He was 15. A few years later he was flying Navy combat jets in Korea. And then he became a test pilot. The test pilot's gig is at least as dangerous as flying combat. Think about it. An airplane designer geek does all kinds of math, and runs wind tunnel tests, then he turns his brand new, untried jet hot rod airplane over to the test pilot and says, "Here. I think this will work ok. Why don't I go hide in a bunker while you go fly it and we'll see."

I'm a pilot too. Certainly not in Neil Armstrong's league. But all pilots have a little kid inside who can't help saying "Whoopiee...look at this...I'm flying." It's the thing that makes us want to be pilots. It's wonderful. We're all three year olds wearing Ray Ban sunglasses. And we all have the same kind of un-forgettable memories of flying times when we wondered, "What the heck am I doing here?" My first flying "What am I doing here" moment actually took place on my very first flight lesson, when the little airplane went zooming down the runway, and I could feel the wheels lifting from the ground.

But somehow I don't think "What am I doing here" is a big enough thought to cover the kind of wonderment that must have been going on in Neil Armstrong's mind as he opened the hatch of Apollo 11 and looked down at the surface of the moon, just a few feet away. And then it was time for, "One small step for a man, one giant leap for mankind." Wow.

It was Buzz Aldrin's "What am I doing here?...Wow," turn next.

Michael Collins must have had a very different kind of "What am I doing here" thought going through his mind. He made the trip all the way from the earth, but he had to stay up in moon orbit to pilot the return rocket, so he came all that way, but he never got to set foot on the moon. I'll bet he always wondered what it would have been like. Imagine...all your life thinking, "how wonderful it might have been."

There are all kinds of little wonderful "stuffs" in life. Some people wonder how I can almost always find a good parking spot. I don't have the answer for that, except that I've come to expect it now, and maybe that helps. I used to wonder about what the kids got away with doing behind my back when they were little. I caught them laughing with each other about it lots of times. What they didn't know is that I also did stuff behind their backs. My Lady Wonder Wench and I weren't always just taking a nap.

And don't you ever wonder what will happen when you die, and friends and relatives will have to go through your stuff? I mean what will they find that will make them laugh. What will they find that might shock them? What will they find that might break their hearts? And I wonder if whoever wrote Twinkle Twinkle Little Star realized it's the same tune as the alphabet song. Think about it. And don't you wonder why the letters are in that ABC order, instead of some other order like Z E G F U L Y...or any other order. And did whoever put the letters in that ABC order had any idea how much of an impact that was going to have on our lives? Can you imagine trying to use a telephone book that's not in alphabetical order?

It's the wonder in our lives that keeps our Louie-Louie Generation happy, healthy and hot.

Three year olds love to wonder...including the ones who put on Ray Ban sunglasses and go flying. And it seems to run in their families. When Neil Armstrong's family announced his death, they said: "For those who may ask what they can do to honor Neil, we have a simple request. Honor his example of service, accomplishment and modesty, and the next time you walk outside on a clear night and see the moon smiling down at you, think of him and give him a wink." The Dreary Drones won't do that. Too un-dignified. And the Pimple People are too busy texting.

But little Cecelia, our daughter Kris, and my Lady Wonder Wench went out in the yard with me last night and we all winked at the moon. Little Cecelia winked with both eyes. And then very softly and carefully, we sang that song together...Twinkle twinkle little star, How I wonder what you are.

It was...wonderful

58-

Smudge

We're coming to the end, and I have one last request. I'll never step on the moon like Neil Armstrong. I'll never win a triathlon. My big audience network radio days are behind me. I'll never make a big mark on life. But maybe I can make a small smudge. In one of my "lovin' touch" books, I said, "Look at life one person at a time." I think Big Louie would approve of that statement. It's got Louie Louie Generation 'Tude." And it takes guts, because it bucks the system. So I'd appreciate it if you'd help me make a small smudge in life here.

The next time you hear about a woman who is somebody's mistress, before you jump to any quick conclusions, take a good, hard look at the lives of each of the people involved, one at a time.

My Lady Wonder Wench has been around horses all her life. She knows a couple of wives who stay with their husbands simply because the guys have money and the women want to keep their fancy, expensive horses. I know one of those husbands, and he's admitted to me that he has a mistress. They really love each other. He doesn't give his mistress money or jewelry or fancy stuff. She doesn't want it anyway. There's nothing that money can buy between them.

Just love. Lusty, sweaty, soul scorching love. I think she deserves respect. I'm not sure I'd say the same for the wife involved.

One of the fascinating stories that came from that rescue of the miners in Chile a few years ago was that some of them had mistresses. The media didn't talk about the mistresses much. That would have caused problems with the Politically Correct Forces for Good in the Community. Mistresses are a little like Stepmothers—they don't get much respect. And that's bizarre, because they sometimes become stepmothers. Not usually. But sometimes.

Think about the chance a woman takes when she becomes a mistress just because she loves a man. I'm not talking about mistress-ing for money. I mean mistress-ing for love. I don't mean a woman who likes to romp with a regiment. I mean a mistress who puts her youth, her reputation, and her beauty at risk, just because she loves one man. She knows going in that a mistress usually loses everything.

Of course, sometimes—not often, but sometimes—she does win. It's a long shot, but sometimes something wonderful happens for both the woman and the man involved. Louie -Louie gentlemen like to come clean. So, as you might have figured out by now, I had a mistress like that. A beautiful young woman full of love, and joy, and dignity.

I'll never step on the moon or win a triathlon or talk to the whole country on network radio again. I'll never make a big mark on life. But please help me make my little smudge. What I'm asking you to do is simple, but it's kind of hard. Because it goes against the flow.

Any time you might remember me, I'd like it to be as one of the people who got you to look at life one person at a time, in that young woman's honor.

She is now my Lady Wonder Wench.

Dick Summer's website is at dicksummer.com

Dick's free weekly podcasts are at dicksummer.com/podcast

Dick's free weekly blog is at dicksummer.com/dsblog

His spoken word with music Personal Audio story albums are:

lovin' touch

Bedtime Stories

Quiet Hands

Night Connections

Night Connections 2

Night Connections 3

Among other places, they are available at Amazon.com and CDBaby.com